Cambridge Elements ≡

Elements in Popular Music
edited by
Rupert Till
University of Huddersfield

THE CROSSINGS

Defining *Slave to the Rhythm*

Jeremy J. Wells
University of York

CAMBRIDGE
UNIVERSITY PRESS

Shaftesbury Road, Cambridge CB2 8EA, United Kingdom

One Liberty Plaza, 20th Floor, New York, NY 10006, USA

477 Williamstown Road, Port Melbourne, VIC 3207, Australia

314–321, 3rd Floor, Plot 3, Splendor Forum, Jasola District Centre,
New Delhi – 110025, India

103 Penang Road, #05–06/07, Visioncrest Commercial, Singapore 238467

Cambridge University Press is part of Cambridge University Press & Assessment,
a department of the University of Cambridge.

We share the University's mission to contribute to society through the pursuit of
education, learning and research at the highest international levels of excellence.

www.cambridge.org
Information on this title: www.cambridge.org/9781009454438

DOI: 10.1017/9781009071079

First published 2023

A catalogue record for this publication is available from the British Library

ISBN 978-1-009-45443-8 Hardback
ISBN 978-1-009-06908-3 Paperback
ISSN 2634-2472 (online)
ISSN 2634-2464 (print)

The Crossings

Defining *Slave to the Rhythm*

Elements in Popular Music

DOI: 10.1017/9781009071079
First published online: October 2023

Jeremy J. Wells
University of York

Author for correspondence: Jeremy J. Wells, jez.wells@york.ac.uk

Abstract: The album Slave to the Rhythm is typical of the exaltation of pop stars but atypical in its presentation and interaction with biographical material. Three crossings are considered in this assessment of the work: technological, cultural and structural. These are presented with a detailed track-by-track analysis using a range of signal processing techniques, some adapted specifically for this project. This Element focuses on the combination of digital, novel and analogue technology that was used and the organisational and transformational treatments of recorded material it offered, along with their associated musical cultures. The way in which studio technology functions, and offers interaction with its users, has a direct influence over the sound of the music that is created with it. To understand how that influence is manifested in *Slave*, there is considerable focus on the development and use of music technology.

Keywords: pop production, musicology, music technology, sampling, Trevor Horn

ISBNs: 9781009454438 (HB), 9781009069083 (PB), 9781009071079 (OC)
ISSNs: 2634-2472 (online), 2634-2464 (print)

Contents

1 Introduction

1.1 The Creation of *Slave to the Rhythm*

Slave to the Rhythm is an audio production first released in 1985, with a second edition appearing in 1987. The sole credited artist is Grace Jones, but, typically for a pop record, there were many musicians, technicians and music-technologists responsible for its creation who are only credited in the liner notes accompanying the physical product. At the time of its release, Grace Jones, also a model and actor, was at the height of her fame. The project was initially intended to be a single, a joint release by the label she was joining (Capitol) and the one she was leaving (Island). This transition between labels is one of the many crossings in the midst of which the record occurs.

That the project grew from this initial plan to become an entire long-playing record is largely due to its producer, Trevor Horn. Horn was 'the most famous record producer in the world at that particular point' (Horn in Warner, 2003, p. 156). He achieved particular critical and commercial success during the 1980s, producing acts such as Frankie Goes to Hollywood, ABC, Propaganda and Yes (of which he was also a member). That success continued into the 1990s with Seal, Robbie Williams and others. Horn is a much-studied record producer. There is at least one book that is dedicated to his work and methods (Warner, 2003), and he is prominent in many other studies of the culture and process of pop music production (e.g. Bennett, 2019 and Cunningham, 1998).

Much of Horn's work has been demanding of both music technology and music performers, striving for perfection rather than the capture of a moment in time, and the time (nine months) spent on *Slave* is a prime example of this. Horn's assistant producer on *Slave* and many other projects in the early and mid-eighties was Steve Lipson:

> Really, the whole album is a collection of experiments in which we were trying to create a good single. The way that worked was that we would have something which was OK, but just not good enough to be a single. Trevor would have a bit of doubt, and I'd say: 'Oh, yeah, great. I'll start again', . . . So Trevor gave me a week. After a week Trevor would come back and say: 'Oh, yeah, that sounds good'. So we'd go back into the studio, look at it, and then suddenly he'd say: 'No, no, no, not really. How about if . . . ?' And I'd work again on it for another week. (Lipson in Tingen, 1987, p. 55)

Horn has referred to the result as the 'ultimate twelve-inch mix' (Horn in Cunningham, 1998, p. 308). It is an album of eight individually titled tracks, yet there is significant sharing of material between those tracks. Despite this commonality between any track on the record and some others, there are some combinations of tracks that do not have any correlation with each other.

This stretches the commonly accepted idea of the 'twelve-inch mix' somewhat. Whether by design or accident but certainly by technology and process, as is described in the following pages, this record seems to exist somewhere between concept album and extended single (another crossing).

All of this, coupled with the fact that the original song on which the album is based was written, by Bruce Woolley and Simon Darlow, for a different act (Frankie Goes to Hollywood), implies an interchangeability, transferability and modularity of the material from which it is constructed. Jones' time (nine hours) spent contributing to the audio of the production is tiny compared to that expended by Lipson and Horn, and yet, as a persona, she is a strongly unifying element of the album. There is a fascinating and unusual weaving and manipulation of common material throughout the record that occurs within the more traditional categories of melody, rhythm and so on but also at the 'signal' level, which is only possible in a produced audio artefact mediated by recording technology.

The record was Jones' most commercially successful album release (excepting the *Island Life* 'greatest hits' compilation) and is amongst Horn's, but the financial expense was great. 'It would take until the end of time to have paid [the production cost] even if it was a number one single all over the world; it was a relative success but not a complete smash hit' (Jones, 2015, p. 301). In terms of critical regard, its resonance has grown over time. Its combination of tracks that are neither solely remixes of the same material nor entirely independent pieces gives rise to a very interesting overall form and one that is not unlike some art music in its repeated, yet thorough, use of material.

Slave is worthy of study, and this Element offers an analysis of this both typical and unusual record. It considers its contexts (both cultural and technological) as well as its form and format and does so by considering its crossings: the ways in which it exists across various continua in which we consider music-making and music artefacts.

1.2 Music and Records

This is an Element about a pop record. This is not much of a surprise in a series on popular music, but the two words 'pop' and 'record' require some careful unpicking in these pages.

Before the arrival of sound recording and reproduction, about a century and a half ago, experiencing music required listening to the live performance of a spontaneous or premeditated (often in the form of a score) composition. With recording came the ability to capture not just the performance instructions (pitches, timing, indications of expression etc.) for music, as in a score, but the actual sound itself (Frith, 1998).

Sound recording is a means for capturing the variations in atmospheric pressure created by the sounding objects (instruments in the case of musical sound) and their operators (players) in the environment (venue), which can then be subsequently reproduced without the need for those objects, players or venue to be present. In that sense, a 'record' is just that: information about a performance by some players in a space.

The final stage of the reproduction chain for recorded sound in a modern audio system is the drive unit in the listener's loudspeaker or headphones, usually an electromagnet connected to a diaphragm. The electromagnet moves backwards and forwards, according to the changing current that flows through its coil of wire, and the diaphragm creates negative and positive variations in pressure that travel through the air and reach our ears to be perceived as sound.

Loudspeakers and headphones are remarkable. They don't look like a piano, or a singer, or a drum, or a set of clapping hands, and yet, without even appearing to move, they can sound like all of those things or any other sounding object that we can call to mind, separately or in any combination. Any sound that we can hear, they can make. We can listen to a recording and say 'that is a voice', or 'that is Elvis Presley's voice', or 'that is Presley's voice in the reverberation of a large chamber'.

Yet, as Magritte's *The Treachery of Images* illustrates (whilst most emphatically not showing an actual pipe), even if a representation enables us very specifically to imagine or verbally state the thing that it is a representation of, it is demonstrably not that thing itself (Magritte, 1929). So whilst loudspeakers can produce any kind of sound, they cannot exactly reproduce the behaviour of sounding objects and spaces. When we talk about capturing the sound of a performance, all that we are capturing are the pressure variations caught by the microphones at the point in space in which they reside, and nothing else. That is what happens when performed music becomes an audio recording. The extent to which recordings can capture and contain the essence of music performances is the subject of much debate (see for example the final two chapters of Cook, 2013).

There is a flip side to all of this. Whilst our audio recording cannot be exactly a musical event that happened, it is also the case that it need not be. There is no need to be constrained to generating any particular type of sound or combining sounds in any particular way. Just as images may depict physical objects to a greater or lesser extent, audio does not have to conform to the laws of acoustics until it leaves the loudspeaker. Before that it can be modified, and even generated from scratch, outside of the acoustic realm. We need not be limited to *repro*duction of sound; we can use these technologies for *pro*duction.

As technologies for storing and reproduction of sound have developed, so have the possibilities for audio creation, modification and reorganisation. Since the advent of magnetic tape and its rapid adoption just after World War II, it has been straightforward to create composite audio signals containing elements that need not have occurred simultaneously or in the order in which they were captured or created. Over this time, a complex relationship has grown up between the techniques and technologies of the studio and other musical activities (the things we might traditionally refer to as composition and performance), to the extent that these things, particularly with pop music and certain forms of art music, are no longer separable. Studio craft is not a separate discipline that occurs alongside the making of music; it is part of it, not an adjunct to it. This idea is central to this Element.

A major subsequent technological change, from both a practical and an economic view, occurred three to four decades later. This was the shift from representing and dealing with audio as some kind of continuously varying analogue of air pressure variations to encoding it as discrete data. *Slave to the Rhythm* was released in 1985, in the middle of this transition. The first crossing that we consider is the shift from analogue to digital that was occurring at the time of its production, which can be observed within the production itself.

Acoustic music, like much of that in the western art music canon, can exist outside of modern technology. Provided the audience is present in a suitable venue (such as a concert hall) at the time of the performance, no loudspeakers or electricity are required for its audition. Within this tradition composers communicate their intentions to performers via a score, a notation that indicates to performers what instruments and pitches they should play and at what moments, with (perhaps) more vague instructions with regard to elements of the performance, such as the quality of tone to be produced, the loudness, the tempo and its malleability. With this set of instructions, interpreted through enculturation in performance practice tradition, the musicians perform the score within an appropriate acoustic space such as a concert hall or a church. The two ears of the listener can be replaced with at least two (and often many more) microphones. The interactions with the performers and the environment are now lost, but the sound field is captured at the points where the microphones are present, and that can be relayed to listeners who now have the freedom to be in different places and different times.

The context of this classical (or acoustic art) music is the concert hall, and what is captured in recordings is presented as giving an impression of the simultaneous performance by the players of the composer's score in that space. That is not to say that classical music productions are an honest portrait of how a performance has been rendered. Human performers make mistakes, wrong notes are played, players fall out of synchronisation with each other, page turns of the score can be noisy and piano stools often creak. This is usually dealt with by editing (something that only became possible with the arrival of tape as a recording medium). On a single album of classical music there may be hundreds of edits, but the listener is not aware of their existence (and if they are, it usually means that the editor has failed in their job).

A common contemporary approach to recording classical music is to use multiple microphones, perhaps as many microphones as there are instruments, positioned close to them. This offers a sound that is recognisable as those instruments, but not in the way that we would hear them were we in the hall. This leads to an impossibly vivid, hyperreal sound, but it rarely occurs to inexpert listeners that this enhanced, artificial clarity is not an honest depiction of the sound being made in that venue. This fakery, to create the impression of natural perfection delivered with impossible clarity, is what Georgina Born describes as a 'realist sonic discourse … in which the goal has been a finished recording that appears simply to capture, and to be faithful to, a prior musical event' and yet 'in which illusionism and realism are emphatic-ally not in contradiction' (Born, 2009, p. 294).

By contrast, much pop music (although not all, as Born points out) is more overtly bound to the processes of recording and post-production. Its illusionism can be obvious. It doesn't concern us when we listen to a Joni Mitchell song that her voice is somehow magically providing a four-part harmony simultaneously with her lead vocal. We don't mind acoustically impossible effects being applied to sounds. We are happy for technique and technology to obviously interfere to creative effect with what we are hearing in pop and (to a lesser extent) rock music.

It is important to note that these are quite crude distinctions, and the musics discussed so far can exist anywhere on a continuum. It is not the case that all pop music exists at one end of that continuum, with acoustic art music at the other end with rock in the middle, but their distributions tend towards these areas. For rock music, Moore highlights attributes of 'intimacy (just Joni Mitchell and her zither) and immediacy (in the sense of unmediated forms of sound production)' (Moore, 2001, p. 199) as being desirable in much of this genre. However, the multitrack layering of her voice, although contributing to the intimacy ('just Joni', no one else), is an obvious impossibility that hardly ever occurs in acoustic art music production; operatic tenors, for example, do not duet with themselves via over-dubbing.

Often (although not always) the audio artefact, the signal on the record that results from the production process, contains things that could not have been acoustically performed and/or performed simultaneously. Even though the audio artefact of a classical record production is not the same as the actual performance in the space, it attempts (often by fakery, as Born notes) to be faithful to some idealised version of the sound of those performers rendering that score in that space sound like. Arguably, the composer's score is central to this musical ideal. It is the document that, when passed through the training and sensitivities of the performers and reverberated in the recording venue, we recognise and hear the essence of as we sit between the loudspeakers to listen. When we think of a Beethoven piano sonata or a Bach concerto, it is typically the score that is thought of, the text from which the music arises and without which it cannot exist.

For many pop productions there is no such text. Yes, there is the song, but that may exist in written form as just a vocal line, lyrics and supporting harmony in tablature form. Besides that, it may exist, as folk music typically did before the widespread collection and notation of songs, as an aural/oral idea passed between the musicians during rehearsals and demo recordings. Then it begins to exist as audio signals, usually not assembled simultaneously in a single performance but rather overlaid and edited with each other and subsequently modified and mixed. Here the editing is not to some pre-existing map (the score), but it is part of the composing process. The modifying and mixing of the different layers of signals is arrangement, but it occurs post hoc rather than to represent an orchestration already explicitly notated in a score.

Often in pop music, the composition process is at least partly contained within the production process. For example, Moorefield describes how the role of 'producer as composer' developed (Moorefield, 2005), although there is also criticism of his 'teleological' explanation of how this concept came into being (Moore, 2007, pp. 127–9). Distinctive sonic signatures emerge as part of the production process and its tools (Zagorski-Thomas, 2014, pp. 49–69). If, as I stated earlier, studio craft is a musical process and not simply a technological adjunct to it, then the text that contains its essence is the specific instantiation of it that exists in the captured and stored audio signal that is the outcome of the production process. The musical text that is *Slave* is the recording itself.

Therefore, many of the analyses in the Element are of the audio itself. The digital data of the recording are measured and visualised, because those data are the fabric of the music and key to understanding its nature and structure. As well as appearing in multiple formats (vinyl disk, cassette etc.), *Slave* also appears in two editions, the first released in 1985 and the second appearing two years later (Jones, 1985c and 1987). The second edition is sometimes referred to as the 'abridged' version, and it is certainly shorter: some of the spoken word inter-ludes between tracks (or movements, as I will refer to them from now on) are removed entirely, and some movements are shorter. This is unusual for pop music, though less so for classical music (Stravinsky, for example, continued to revise *The Rite of Spring* for many years after its first performance) and also not unheard of for Trevor Horn productions. For example, there are two editions of Seal's first album, produced by Horn, even with identical catalogue numbers.[1] It is commonplace for differently mastered versions of records to be released, and many records have been reissued with additional material, such as remixes or demo versions, appended to the original structure of the work. Songs often appear in different forms as remixes, but these are usually differentiated from each other via different names (e.g. the 'Carnage', 'Annihilation' etc. – remixes of Frankie Goes to Hollywood's 'Two Tribes'). What is unusual in the case of *Slave* and the Seal reissue is that there is nothing to differentiate the two editions of this record outside of the track ordering and the audio content itself, as if the creators did not want to draw attention to the fact and it was a revision intended to replace, rather than exist alongside, the original version (and that was the reason reportedly given by Seal for two different versions of his debut album). The edition of *Slave* that is analysed here is the second (1987) edition.

There are also other stark differences that seem to exist between the two clusterings of music that we refer to as classical (or art) and pop music. I use the term 'seem' deliberately, since they are not universally accepted, and counterexamples can usually be found. Here I argue that *Slave* is one such counterexample. In some ways it represents a middle ground, and in others it is a plurality, belonging to those two broad clusters of pop and classical simultaneously. An example of this is the way that it uses material. From a pop perspective it might be seen as mainly a collection of remixes of the same song; from an art music perspective it might be seen as an integrated long-form work with the same material, sometimes altered, appearing in different movements.

The rest of this Element is structured as follows. In the next section an overview of the technological developments in sound recording and music production is given along with how *Slave* is positioned at the crossing between analogue and digital technology. This section is also important foundation material for the track-by-track analysis that follows in Section 3. It is intended to give the reader a general overview of the important issues that are relevant to the subsequent discussion. Some readers may already be familiar with this material but, given the multidisciplinary nature of music technology, there may be some who are not. This is then followed by two other crossings that the Element considers: the cultures within which *Slave* came into being and that it embodies, and the final form(s) that its music takes.

---

[1] http://futureloveparadise.co.uk/anthology/disc-album/seal1edit.html.

2 Crossing One: Technology

> The recording studio is a musical instrument ... In the seventies it was still a recording studio because you had to play everything but then, suddenly, in the eighties it started to change and the studio literally became an instrument.
>
> Trevor Horn[2]

This quote ignores work stretching back through the 1970s that had explored expression through studio technology such as that by Brian Eno, discussed in Eno (2004), and dub producers such as King Tubby (Milner, 2009, pp. 301–8) and, of course, George Martin and The Beatles. However, it does identify a moment when a paradigmatic shift in how sound was organised and controlled in the studio was taking place, which occurred as Horn was creating his most notorious work. This section summarises this shift, and the major relevant technologies that feature in *Slave* are presented. Some audio analysis methods used in the following section are also introduced.

2.1 Delaying Sound

Hearing delayed repetitions of sounds is part of every listening experience. Unless we are in an anechoic chamber, sounds that arrive at our ears do so via multiple paths. Any object or surface will reflect sound to a greater or lesser extent: reflection of sound energy happens whenever there is a change in the medium through which it is travelling. The first sound to arrive at the listener is that which has travelled the shortest distance. Where there are no other objects between the listener and sounding object, this is known as the direct sound. Other paths, where sound has arrived after interacting with an object or objects in some way (diffraction or reflection), are travelled by indirect sound. Because these indirect paths are not as the crow flies, they are longer than the direct path, and these waves reach the listener later than those that follow the direct path (Angus and Howard, 2009).

The duration of the delay between the direct and indirect sound arriving determines how it affects our perception. If the time of arrival (TOA) difference is more than about 100 ms, then the second arrival is heard as a separate and distinct event, an echo. If it is much less than this, the second arrival is perceptually fused with the first. If the TOA difference is above 50 ms, then it is the temporal quality of the combined sound that we hear as different, and the sound appears to be louder. Below around 50 ms (which is the time taken for an oscillation of a 20 Hz wave – the lowest frequency of pressure variation that we perceive as a single pitch), it is the spectral quality of sound that is altered. In

---

this region the different path lengths cause cancellation (a positive pressure wave meeting a negative one) and reinforcement (a negative meeting a negative, or a positive meeting a positive) effects at particular frequencies in a spectral pattern known as a comb filter (Borwick, 1990).

The speed of sound in air in typical atmospheric conditions is about 340 m per second (Bass et al., 1995). So the distance to a surface (e.g. a wall) that will take 200 ms to reflect sound back (100 ms to travel to the surface to you, another 100 ms to travel back) is 34 m or more, which is almost one and a half times the length of a tennis court. Introducing delays into sound, particularly ones that can be adjusted, is not feasible in the acoustic domain because of the distances involved for even quite short delays and for various other practical reasons.

This relationship between the short delays, and the large distances that they imply, can create the impression of impressively large landscapes or structures. The slap-back echo is a distinctive quality of rockabilly productions from the 1950s (Lacasse, 2000, pp. 122–6). Listening to Elvis Presley's 'Blue Moon of Kentucky', there is a particular (and arguably impressive) quality to Presley's voice lent by the addition of a single, slightly delayed copy of the sound to the original signal (Presley, 1954). It sounds as if Presley is being heard over a long distance, as if his is the only voice that is permitted to be heard within a very large space that perhaps lends an additional importance to the voice and to the desirability of its owner.

We can use a signal analysis technique, called autocorrelation, to estimate the delay times used in recordings. The similarity, or cross-correlation, between two signals can be calculated by multiplying their amplitudes together at points along their length. For digital signals, the amplitude values of each corresponding sample in the two signals are multiplied, and then all of the outcomes of these multiplications are added together. If the resultant number is zero or close to zero, then the signals are completely uncorrelated, or close to it. If the number is big and positive, then the signals are highly correlated. If the number is big and negative, then the signals are highly correlated but one is the mirror image of the other (i.e. they are 'out of phase'). This correlation can be calculated with different shifts (delays or lags, as they are often referred to in the signal analysis literature). If, instead of two different signals, this operation is done with two copies of the same signal, then it becomes autocorrelation, and measuring this at different lags shows us at what lags the signal is most similar to itself (Smith, 2011).

Figure 1 shows the waveform of 'Blue Moon of Kentucky'. This is the typical visual representation of audio that we see in audio software, with time on the horizontal axis and the amplitude (with arbitrary units where −1.0 and +1.0 are the maximum possible negative and positive signal levels).

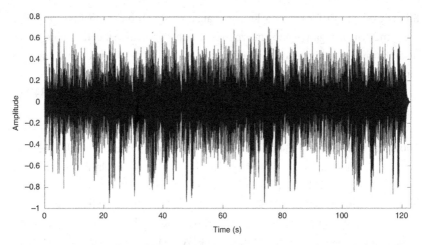

Figure 1 Time-domain waveform of 'Blue Moon of Kentucky' – Elvis Presley
(Sun Records, 1954).

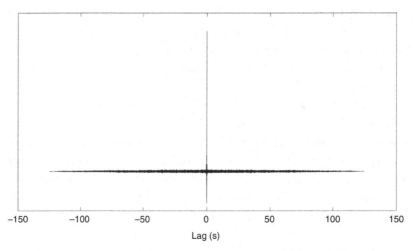

Figure 2 Autocorrelation of 'Blue Moon of Kentucky' – Elvis Presley
(Sun Records, 1954).

Figure 2 shows a plot of autocorrelation values measured at different shifts of
the signal with itself.

Notice that there are positive and negative lags and the pattern of values is
symmetric around zero. Notice also that there is a very strong and narrow peak
in the values at zero. This is because when the lag between a signal and itself is
zero, there is perfect correlation. Figure 3 shows the same autocorrelation plot,
but zoomed into a much smaller range of lag values.

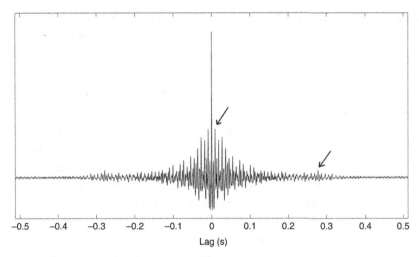

Figure 3 Zoomed autocorrelation of 'Blue Moon of Kentucky' – Elvis Presley (Sun Records, 1954).

A general pattern can be seen of the similarity decreasing as the lag increases. The fluctuations that can be seen are mainly due to pitched components. The song is recorded in the key of A, and the larger peaks close to zero show the lags that represent a single period of A. The peak indicated by the short arrow corresponds to a single cycle of 220.5 Hz, which is slightly sharp of the A below middle C. Sustained notes at specific pitches create signals that are self-similar when they are delayed by one period (the time taken for a complete oscillation) of the waveform or integer multiples of it.

At longer lags self-similarity results from repetition due to rhythm and, in this case, the use of slap-back delay. The longer arrow in Figure 3 points to a subtle deviation from the general pattern of decaying similarity due to the use of the delay. The peak of this deviation occurs at a lag of 278 ms and gives us an accurate estimate of the delay applied during this recording. This equates to a distance travelled of nearly 100 m. But in this case, the sound of Presley's voice being impressively present in an enormous space is a fiction afforded by analogue recording technology. What we are hearing is the delay between tape passing between the record and replay heads of a single analogue tape machine. The distance between the two is about two inches, and the tape is travelling at 7½ inches per second. An enormous physical space is evoked by a much smaller machine.

2.2 Towards the Sampler

Digital storage of sound enabled a further leap in miniaturisation and flexibility. The sampler has precursor technology in tape recording (Davis, 1996, pp. 7–8) and then the digital delay line (Blesser, 1971). In 1979, Advanced Music

Systems (AMS), based in Burnley in the north-west of England, launched the DMX15-80 microprocessor-controlled digital delay. Sarm Studios, owned by Trevor Horn and his wife Jill Sinclair, where *Slave* was mixed, had these delay units installed. Instead of using shift registers to pass audio data down a series of storage devices, moving through each one a sample at a time, the DMX15-80 used random access memory (RAM). This meant that data could be placed and read from anywhere in memory by the processor. So, rather than simply being a device whose delay could be user-adjusted via a dial on the front panel, this was a device that could remember and instantly recall different configurations.

Rather than the digital audio samples shifting down a line of registers, whose input and output points were fixed and internal states were not readily accessible, they remained in the memory locations in which they were initially placed; it was the input (memory write) and output (memory read) locations that changed. This enabled the distance between input and output points to be dynamically altered. The delay was no longer a pipe with an input at one end and an output at the other; it was a store of samples that could be written to and read from at any memory location.

In late 1979, a single unit of RAM with 64 kilobytes of space (enough to store about 50 ms of stereo audio at CD quality) was available for $419 (McCallum, 2022), equivalent to about $1500 in 2021. Compared to the vast amounts of storage available for a fraction of that amount today, memory was very expensive, but it had already fallen significantly in price per byte since such devices first began to appear in the late 1950s. Whereas digital delay units that offered maximum times similar to that offered by the distance between record and replay heads of repurposed analogue tape machines were financially viable in the early 1970s, by the end of that decade stereo delay units that offered one or two seconds of delay (albeit not yet at the 16 bit and 44.1 kHz quality of the soon-to-arrive CD) were becoming viable.

The flexibility of this RAM and processor-based unit offered a functionality that took it beyond just the delaying of signals. It offered a lock-in function. When the lock-in switch on the unit was activated, the contents of the RAM were retained, replacing samples in memory with new ones from the device's input halted, and the output of the unit was produced by reading through all of the stored samples in sequence and then repeating this process ad infinitum until the lock-in switch was turned off. The manual that AMS supplied with the stereo version of the unit encouraged users to 'think of it as two tape recorders with the ability to create instant tape loops, the initial loop size being governed by the maximum storage capability of the delay lines' (Advanced Music Systems, 1978). The start and end points of these loops could then be edited using the front panel controls. It was also possible to trigger the sound stored in

RAM, with their edited start and end points, to play at any time, making the unit, in effect, a digital sampler.

AMS also launched one of the first digital reverberators in 1981. Essentially a network of a few, short digital delays, it offered a convincing alternative to the plate reverberators that were then in common use in studios (BBC Engineering, 1963). Additionally, it offered simulations of rooms, such as churches and concert halls and, famously, non-linear programs that offered reverberation with implausible time envelopes such as the gated reverb effect heard extensively in Prince's mid-eighties work, such as 'Kiss' (Prince, 1986), where it is applied to the kick drum (Buskin, 2013). These devices were expensive but took up far less space than plate reverberators and offered a range of possibilities: plates, rooms and fantastic treatments of sound that had no parallel in the acoustic or mechanical realms.

The word sampling has two meanings in audio. The first relates to the capture at instants in time of an audio signal for quantisation as part of the analogue to digital conversion process (Watkinson, 2000). The second refers to capture of entire sounds, from an instrument note to an entire passage of music, for use as material within a separate work. Because of the practical differences in the flexible capture, storage and replay of audio between analogue and digital devices, music sampling is predominantly something that has occurred within digital technology, but some analogue forms of this instrument did exist.

A 1927 patent by Frank Robb described a musical instrument that could play looped recordings of instruments from rotating cylinders but the recordings could not be changed (Murphy and Anstey, 2020). Some twenty years later, Pierre Schaeffer's *musique concrete* manipulated recordings of sound from which to create new collages, in the studios of the French broadcaster RTF. However, these were created via direct interaction with the recording media (e.g. by cutting and splicing tape) or assembled and arranged by recording these media onto a final medium. In other words, these samples of existing sound were not played from a musical instrument interface but either arranged offline (i.e. not in real time) or realised in real-time as the human-coordinated playback of multiple replay devices. This latter approach has been described as approaching the functionality of a sampler: 'Indeed he developed a great facility in the studio for "performing" the playback and level controls of several (often four) playback turntables for creating his early sound collages, thus putting together – especially if the disks contained more than one closed groove[3] – a type of sampling machine' (Davies, 1996).

---

[3] A closed groove on a (what would have then been shellac, and what would now be vinyl) disk is one in which the end runs into the start after a single rotation, and therefore creates an indefinite-

The linear structure of magnetic tape combined with its amenability to structural intervention (i.e. the fact that it could be cut at any point along its length and then joined at another point using nothing more than a razor blade and some sticky tape) meant that temporal relations within recordings could be easily manipulated. Reversed playback could be achieved simply by swapping the two reels of tape and turning them around. These possibilities, coupled with variable speed, enabled recordings of sound to be manipulated and organised in a wide variety of ways. Tape-based pieces were typically constructed offline, but there were some bespoke modifications of machines that enabled some performative elements (Davies, 1996).

The Mellotron M400 (1970) was the most common of a family of instruments that had been developed from an initial concept first realised at the end of the 1940s by Harry Chamberlin and was an instrument that was heard in the recordings of artists from The Beatles to Isao Tomita. The M400 created sound by playing short strips of tape that were activated by playing a keyboard. Although it could be loaded with new sounds, this was a difficult operation, and so it was mainly heard with the original tapes of sound with which it was supplied.

A set of factory-supplied sounds was also provided with the first digital sampling instrument, the Fairlight Computer Musical Instrument (CMI), which appeared in 1979. However, this was a much more straightforward instrument for the user to create their own samples with since, as with the AMS digital delay, this was a microprocessor and RAM-mediated task that did not involve moving parts or loading of mechanisms for each musical note. One sound could be played at different pitches by simply altering the sampling rate of the playback. Since the same sound stored in RAM could be accessed by different rate playbacks, an individual copy was not needed for each note being played. In the same way as the digital delay, storing the sound as bits in memory that could be addressed at any time in any order by a processor, whilst requiring significant technological sophistication,[4] did not require any moving parts, except for the disk drives on which sounds were supplied and stored.

The inventors of the CMI had initially attempted a system for digitally creating, synthesising, sounds from scratch. They found that building sounds from the bottom up using their processor and RAM technology was not yielding

---

duration looped output when played, rather than continuing in a single spiral that travels incrementally inwards to the centre of the disk with each rotation.

[4] Such as the research and development of the metal-oxide-semiconductor transistor that made RAM in the form of integrated circuits (chips) possible. Such technology was developed for computing and communications, far broader applications than professional musical audio, economically justifying the significant investment involved.

results that were interesting enough, so they reluctantly decided to try the cheat of using digital recordings of sound, samples, as the starting point:

> Sampling gave us the complexity of sound that we had failed to create digitally, but not the control we were looking for . . . We regarded using recorded real-life sounds as a compromise – as cheating – and we didn't feel particularly proud of it. (Vogel in Tingen, 1996, p. 49)

The CMI was supplied with a set of floppy disks containing samples of orchestral instruments, and so was similar in intended application to the Mellotron. One advantage of the digital audio stored in RAM approach was that sound playback could be a combination of linear and looped: an issue with the Mellotron was that, in order to have a convincing attack,[5] sounds could not be looped and so were of finite duration – once the tape for a particular key had run out, the sound would stop until the key was released and re-pressed (causing the tape to be quickly returned to its start position via a spring-like mechanism). With random access to audio data, the attack portion of a sound could be played when a key was depressed, followed by a section that looped for as long as the key was held down and then, finally, a release portion once the finger was lifted from the key.

Although this enabled notes of variable length to be created with convincing attack and release, there are many other behaviours of acoustic instruments that the sampler could not recreate. For example, when more energy is injected into an acoustic instrument (i.e. it is played harder), then it does not just get louder, its spectral envelope (the distribution of energy across different frequencies) changes: typically, the sound gets brighter (high frequencies become relatively more dominant). A single monolithic recording of an instrument at a single pitch could not possibly contain all of the information required to explain the behaviour of that instrument at different pitches and dynamics.

However, it did offer a very flexible and musically intuitive (via its keyboard interface) way of interacting with recorded sound, *any* recorded sound. Although the amount of RAM in the first CMI was small by modern standards

---

[5] The evolution of a note from an acoustic instrument is determined in part by how energy is imparted over time (consider the difference in sound between a violin string being plucked and being bowed). The 'attack' portion of a sound occurs when energy input begins. It is followed by the portion through which the energy input is 'sustained' and, finally, by the decay of the sound once the energy input has ceased (the note is 'released'). The Mellotron passed a finite length of tape that contained the recorded attack and sustained and released portions of the sound over its replay head in a linear manner (i.e. once, and at a constant speed). If a tape loop had been used instead, then there would have been no attack or release, just the starting and stopping of a continuous loop of tape. A system that used random access (i.e. any part of it could be accessed at the same speed as any other part) memory meant that an attack portion could be played, followed by a looped sustain portion while the key was depressed, finishing with a release portion when the key was released.

(there were 16 kb of RAM per voice), the sampling rate could be adjusted to allow negotiation between bandwidth and sample length: at the maximum sample rate of 24 kHz, samples were constrained to be less than a second in length (the quantisation resolution was eight bits); at the minimum rate of 8 kHz (which offered the same bandwidth as digital telephony), then a couple of seconds was possible. Peter Gabriel owned the first CMI in the UK, having invited Peter Vogel, one of its inventors, to his studio in the summer of 1979 to give a demonstration when he was recording his third album. Speaking in 1981, during recording sessions for his fourth album, he indicated the prominence that the instrument had in his plans. 'I hope to use the Fairlight to give me some of the unusual soundscapes with which I'm going to try make this record [his fourth solo album, released in 1982] different' (*The South Bank Show*, 1982).

The Series I CMI could capture control (i.e. musical notes and other expressive gestures made by the player) data as well as audio and it offered a scripting language for creating and editing that data, known as MCL (music control language). The CMI Series II was released in 1982 (for £30,000, which would be about £110,000 now) and offered a new approach for editing control data, known as 'Page R'. According to J. J. Jeczalik, Art of Noise member and Fairlight programmer, 'Page R transformed the whole machine' (Jeczalik in Anniss, 2016). It was now possible to create 'sequences' of notes playing specific sounds at specific times and easily copy these to create song structures. Events could be 'quantised' to the nearest musical time value (e.g. something that had been played behind the beat could be moved exactly on to it), a feature that was born out of necessity, since the system could not keep up with real-time input (Gardner, 2012).

This rhythmic quantisation is as much a part of the new sound of digital music as sampling was, for better or worse. Asked in 1987 about why he had used a real brass section to play on his single 'Sledgehammer' and not just used a sample, Gabriel said, 'I think there's still something magical that happens when you get the interaction between live players. No amount of good programming can replace that. As I hear more and more bands based completely around drum machines and sequencers, I pine to hear more musicians playing with each other' (Gabriel in Hammond, 1987, p. 41). As discussed in the following section, *Slave* is an interesting hybrid of human playing and computer sequencing. By the time of Gabriel's interview, the final incarnation of the CMI, the Series III, which offered CD quality digital audio with 44.1 kHz sampling and 16-bit quantisation, had been available for two years. It was launched at a retail price of £60,000 (the equivalent of £190,000 today).

2.3 Workstations for Sound

The Fairlight system was not the only instrument available for sampling in the early 1980s. In the United States, the New England Digital (NED) company launched the first version of their Synclavier digital musical instrument in 1978. As was the case for Fairlight, the original intention for this instrument was not sampling, but digital synthesis of sounds from scratch. To that end, NED had licensed frequency modulation (FM) synthesis from Yamaha (who, in turn, had licensed the technology from Stanford University).

Both additive and FM are synthesis methods that are based on sinusoidal waveforms. Sinusoids are considered a fundamental building block of sounds because they are the simplest form of vibration, existing at only one frequency. Additive synthesis, as the name suggests, constructs sounds by adding together sine waves of different frequencies and amplitudes. To accurately synthesise sounds (particularly at onsets, where energy often exists at a number of different frequencies), a large number of sinusoidal oscillators can be required. Rather than being additive, FM is multiplicative, in the sense that one oscillator's amplitude is used to modulate the frequency of another 'carrier' oscillator. John Chowning showed how a wide variety of both harmonic and inharmonic sounds could be created with very rich spectra via this method (Chowning, 1973).

Despite Fairlight's aborted attempt at creating an additive digital synthesiser, they did retain this functionality in the CMI, in addition to its sampling capability. However, it was FM that was the first digital synthesis method to have an impact, firstly via the Synclavier I (it could also do additive synthesis) and early adopters such as UK producer Mike Thorne (Flint, 2000), and then much more broadly via the extraordinary success of the Yamaha DX-7, launched in 1983, which made FM cheaply available and whose preset[6] sounds permeated pop records of the 1980s (Lavengood, 2017).

In 1982, sampling functionality was added to the Synclavier II. This used sampling directly to hard disks to offer longer sampling times at then higher (16-bit quantisation, 50 kHz sampling rate) quality. Given then 5 MB capacity of the disk drives, samples of up to 50 seconds in length were possible, although they could only be played one at a time (Electronics and Music Maker, 1983). The RAM plus floppy diskette approach of Fairlight offered flexibility and immediacy but at the cost of short sample times and relatively

---

[6] Editing of sounds on the DX-7 is notoriously difficult, partly because of the abstract nature of FM (the relationship between input parameters and output sound is often not intuitive) and because of its combination of tiny editing display and menu-driven interaction. Hence, few users strayed far from the preprogrammed sounds that Yamaha provided.

poor audio quality because of the low storage capacity of RAM, whereas the straight-to-disk approach of NED offered greater capacity and therefore longer, better quality sampling but lacked some of the immediate 'playability' of the CMI.

A natural extension of 'sample to disk' was 'direct to disk' recording, a term that NED coined in 1986 to describe a facility for using its system in place of a magnetic tape recorder. In an interview, Brad Naples, the vice-president of NED, described its capabilities:

> We have what we call the 'Direct-To-Disk Multitrack Recording System' coming out in May, and this will enable you to record sound directly onto disk memory without the need for audio tape. As it's a completely digital system, you'll be able to manipulate the sound in many ways. For example, you'll be able to slide one track backwards or forwards relative to another, correct tuning or speed the whole song up or down without affecting the pitch – it's entirely flexible.
>
> The effect of introducing such a system means that a person or studio can have a room which doesn't necessarily have to have super-sophisticated and expensive acoustic treatment and racks of fancy effects. It just needs the bare essentials of a good clean mixing console and monitoring system, and then that person can install a Synclavier and make a record from scratch, much quicker and with excellent fidelity. (Naples in Gilby, 1986)

This statement was a bold and clear vision but it, and much more besides, largely came to pass. What Naples was describing is what we would now think of as a digital audio workstation (DAW). DAWs are now the dominant paradigm for music production at all levels of sophistication and expense and are also widely accessible due to the widespread ownership of personal computers as desktops, laptops and, increasingly, tablets and phones, which can host software and connect to audio interfaces that enable them to record, process and mix audio. The Fairlight and NED systems were expensive because, although the integrated circuits they used – such as processors and RAM – were developed within the wider electronics and computing research and development effort, many of the other components (such as analogue-to-digital (ADC) and digital-to-analogue (DAC) converters) were bespoke: they had to be designed and built from scratch for these specific machines (which, incidentally, along with the lower resolution, particularly of the CMI, is one of the reasons that they are considered by Horn, and others, to have a unique sonic character). Now multiple ADCs and DACs are available on single chips (at the time of writing this, a stereo DAC chip is available from Texas Instruments with 24-bit quantisation and a sample rate of 200 kHz, for under three pounds sterling). Additionally, the processing power and memory of computer hardware per unit price has increased exponentially since the 1950s (Nordhaus, 2001).

2.4 Digital Tape

Digital recording was possible before the advent of hard disk-based systems by using magnetic tape. The first digital tape recorder was reported in the *Journal of the Audio Engineering Society* in 1973 by the OKI Electric Industry Company Ltd. It sampled audio at 40 kHz and quantised it using 13 bits (Sato, 1973). By the early eighties, two competing formats had emerged: Mitsubishi's ProDigi and the DASH (digital audio stationary head) format adopted by Sony and Studer. In 1988, Sony described the PCM-3348, a 48-track digital recorder capturing audio at 16 bits and 48 kHz, at the AES' autumn conference in Los Angeles (Urayama et al., 1988).

Whilst digital was attempting to emulate the editing capabilities of analogue, analogue was acquiring an (arguably) improved resolution via advances in noise reduction technology. Ray Dolby described his famous, first noise reduction system for analogue recording in 1967. This system, referred to as Dolby 'A', was aimed at audio recorders for professional purposes (since it required regular alignment of equipment to ensure that recordings could be played back without frequency- and dynamic-varying errors in the level of playback). It offered an improvement in the dynamic range of a recording system of 10 dB, rising to 15 dB between 5 and 15 kHz. The best signal to noise ratio possible with ½" two-track analogue tape machines reached about 70 dB,[7] so the addition of Dolby A could push this to 80 and beyond. Dolby, and some other complementary (or double-ended) noise reduction systems, worked via compansion (a portmanteau of compression and expansion). Low level signals were boosted before being recorded on to tape and then reduced when played back, also reducing the level of the tape noise. High level signals were left untouched, since these masked tape noise anyway. The result was a recording where the audible noise was 10 dB lower in level.

In 1986, a year after *Slave*'s production, just as DASH was beginning to establish itself as the digital tape format of choice, with over 300 units having been sold by that point (Bennet, 2019, p. 27), Ray Dolby described an enhancement of his original Dolby A system, spectral recording (or Dolby SR) to the Audio Engineering Society (Dolby, 1986). In between A and SR, Dolby had devised 'B' (1968) and 'C' (1980) for domestic use. SR offered an improvement in dynamic range of 25 dB at high frequencies, pushing the performance of the very best tape machines into a dynamic range of about 95 dB, which is the equivalent to that of a digital system with 16-bit quantisation. At the time, Dolby's professed preference was for analogue recording.

---

[7] 70 dB is the non-weighted (i.e. linear) figure for ½" at 30 IPS published in the technical specifications of the Studer A820 manual (Studer, 1993).

[Digital] costs a lot of money, it's very complicated, it's the wrong way to do it . . . I don't want to sound confrontational; I'm not out to get the digital guys. But my opinion is that for a while these two systems, SR and digital, will coexist in recording studios. Then sanity will prevail, and the digital systems will fall into disuse. (Dolby in New York Times News Service, 1987)

The first assertion was correct; the latter was utterly wrong. Digital tape machines did fall into disuse (although DASH was used for *Slave*, particularly in the capture and assemblage of the percussion parts) and some use of analogue tape machines continues to this day, but both were largely supplanted by the hard disk recording that the Synclavier II heralded.

It was some time before the DAW was sufficiently cheap and powerful to dominate music production, but the possibilities of systems such as the Synclavier, even in 1985, were enabling those who had access to such equipment to make records in ways that had never been done before, and *Slave* is an example of that.

3 *Slave to the Rhythm*: The Text

As discussed in the first section, *Slave to the Rhythm* (Jones, 1985c and 1987) is an audio production. It is distributed as audio signals for audition via sound reproduction equipment, accompanied by artwork and sleeve-notes. All of these are important and relate to each other. The audio is comprised of sung and spoken word, sounds from acoustic instruments and synthesisers, all with varying degrees of processing applied as part of the production process. As well as being an audio production, *Slave* is also the song that the production presents. As discussed in the next section, this began as something entirely separate from Grace Jones. The exact format of the song in this incarnation is not known, but typically it would consist of a vocal melody with supporting harmonies, probably notated or those elements captured as a simple audio demo (as a way of asserting the rights of its authors, if nothing else).

Melody, harmony, timbre, rhythm, words and images are all combined in the artefact. In the case of this record, the way in which they are created and combined is overtly related to the technologies used for its production. In the previous section, some important and relevant developments in music technology that preceded the production were presented, along with audio analysis tools that enable exploration and understanding of these studio tools and techniques. This is necessary background because so much of the essence of *Slave* is within the way that sound is processed and combined, as well as the sounds that are captured and created. More traditional analytical tools, such as transcriptions of rhythm, harmony and melody, remain relevant and are used throughout the description of *Slave* that comprises this section. Additional audio analysis methods, such as the wavelet transform, are also introduced and explained. The variety of components in this production is reflected in the variety of analytical and presentational tools used in this section, and the relevance of each is explained when they are introduced. These tools are not used in complete isolation from each other. Human audition can check the reliability of computer-made measurements (of tempo, for example), and analytical listening can be usefully enhanced by visualisations and measurements of audio.

In this section, I often refer to Warner's excellent monograph on Trevor Horn, which includes a perceptive and imaginative discussion of *Slave* and is the most detailed analysis of Horn's work to date (Warner, 2003). Because it deals with Horn's entire production career up to *Slave*, its specific coverage of this specific record is less detailed than what I present here. Inspired in part by Warner's analysis, I offer in these pages something that is complementary to that work yet affords more detailed coverage and justification of the audio analysis tools used to inform it. Since Warner's work, the field of music information retrieval has emerged and matured (e.g. Lartillot and Toiviainen, 2007). The tools that this new field brings enable a much more tangible and accessible analysis of works such as *Slave*, and this Element demonstrates how they can be used to create new and meaningful insights into music production.

3.1 Jones the Rhythm

> Rhythm is both the song's manacle and its demonic charge.
>
> Penman (1985)

The first track begins with the actor Ian McShane reading this extract, 'The Annihilation of Rhythm', written by Ian Penman, which also appears in the text on the vinyl sleeve/cassette inlay card/CD booklet. Penman, who wrote for the New Musical Express (NME) in the late seventies and early eighties, was noted for his witty and surreal takes on pop culture. His writing style was not universally popular, even with colleagues: '[Paul] Morley [another NME journalist who conducted interviews with Grace Jones for this project and wrote some of the sleeve notes] always delivered great interviews and Ian was very bright. But their egos went absolutely out of control. They were writing pretentious bullshit' (Long, 2012, p. 141). The use of actors and the spoken word is something of a trademark in Trevor Horn/Steve Lipson productions released on ZTT Records (established by Horn, Jill Sinclair and Morley). Other examples include John Hurt in The Art of Noise's *The Seduction of Claude Debussy* (1999) and Geoffrey Palmer reading Nietzsche for the extended mixes of Frankie Goes to Hollywood's 'Welcome to the Pleasure Dome'. Spoken word had also recently featured in two other highly successful singles: Paul Hardcastle's '19' (Hardcastle, 1985) and Michael Jackson's 'Thriller' (Jackson, 1982).

McShane reports that he was spotted by Trevor Horn in a chip shop in London and invited to do the reading there and then. The two were already long-term acquaintances, but that particular meeting was by chance. When Horn spotted McShane he asked, 'what are you doing after supper? I need a voice and Orson Welles is dead' (Patten, 2019). Orson Welles, as well as being a highly regarded actor and filmmaker, was also a sought-after voiceover actor (well known to UK audiences for his proclaiming Carlsberg to be 'probably the best lager in the world'), capable of a deep and powerful, yet also low intensity, delivery. McShane's voice is similar. Captured in close proximity to the microphone as it is in this recording, it is perhaps best described as a spoken form of baritone crooning. Welles had died on 10 October 1985, and *Slave* is listed as being released on 28 October. This implies that McShane's recording was made within just three weeks of the record's final release. Allowing for post-production and manufacturing time, this is a very short timescale, even if the rest of the project was already completed and mixed prior to the addition of his voice recording.

Figure 4 shows the autocorrelation of the left and right stereo channels. As can be seen from the peaks, the voice is heard with delayed versions of itself in the left (125 ms, one eighth of a second) and right (150 ms). We hear these delayed versions as distinct echoes, and this has a spatial effect: the voice has been placed into an environment, some kind of large space (the echoes are the reflections that we might hear in a very large room: sound travels 50 m in 150 ms). Yet there is something distinctly unnatural about this space: aside from these early reflections, there is no other reverberation. It's hard to imagine what this environment might actually look like. Perhaps we are outdoors in some enormous, semi-enclosed space. Maybe it is 'the mouth's open erotic sky' of Penman's text. At the end of this introduction McShane intones, 'Ladies and Gentlemen, Miss Grace Jones. Jones the rhythm'. The last sentence has no delay applied to it and it is in mono, so there is a sudden shift in perspective: the voice now seems very close and there is no sense that it is in a large room or other space. The changing of the delay applied to the voice in this way is the aural analogue of suddenly zooming in from a distant and wide camera angle to a narrow close-up.

One way of quantifying stereo width is to measure the ratio between what are known as 'mid' and 'side' signals. These signals can be very simply created from the left and right components of a stereo signal: the mid signal is the left

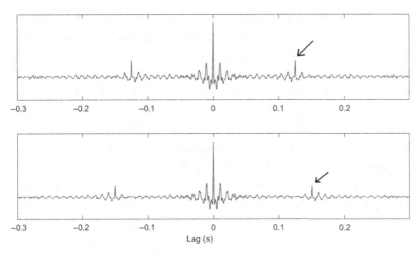

Figure 4 Zoomed autocorrelation, for left (top) and right (bottom) channels, of the opening few seconds of McShane's reading of Penman's *The Annihilation of Rhythm*.

and right signals added to each other, and the side is the left and right signals subtracted from each other. The mid signal is quite an intuitive concept since it is usually what is heard when a stereo signal is played from a mono device; what the side signal represents is not quite so straightforward. Essentially, the mid signal contains all of the elements that are heard emanating from the centre point between the two loudspeakers. Any components that come from that central position are not included in the side signal at all, because they have equal levels in both the left and right loudspeakers and so disappear when one is subtracted from the other. Any components that are either 'fully right' and 'fully left' (i.e. are heard only in one of the loudspeakers) contribute equally to the mid and side signals (Rumsey and McCormick, 2014).

If a component moves from being only in one speaker towards the centre, then the level of the side signal falls and the level of the mid signal rises as this happens. So, what is happening if the level of the mid signal is lower than the side signal? This indicates that there are more 'out of phase' than 'in phase' components in the stereo signal. When signals are completely in phase, then both the left and right loudspeaker diaphragm move outwards and inwards together. When signals are completely out of phase, then, as one diaphragm is moving outwards, the other is moving inwards and vice versa. This creates an arguably unnatural effect, and listeners typically report that imaging (the ability to identify a specific location from which a sound source appears to be located) is vague and sound seems to be coming from outside of the loudspeakers.

Therefore, when a stereo signal is in mono (and it appears to be emanating from a single point that is equidistant between the two loudspeakers), it is deemed to be as 'narrow' as it can be. In this case there is no energy in the side signal, but there is energy in the mid. In the case where there is no energy in the mid signal, but there is in the side, then we have the impression of completely unfocussed sound and it is deemed to be as 'wide' as it can be. Therefore, the ratio of the mid and side signals, usually expressed in decibels (dB), can give a crude measure of stereo width. Traditionally, care has been taken in sound recording and production with this ratio; side signals by definition do not exist in mono reproduction, so stereo signals with high ratios of side to mid energy are often deemed inappropriate for mono delivery and vinyl disks cut with high-energy side signals are more prone to skipping, since the side signal is encoded in the vertical dimension of the stereo groove (mid is encoded in the horizontal dimension) and significant excursions may cause the reproduction stylus to jump out of the groove.

During the section of McShane's monologue that has delays of different duration applied to the left and right channel, the ratio of side to mid signal is about −14 dB (the negative indicates that the energy in the side signal is lower than that of the mid). During the utterance 'Jones the rhythm' (which has the voice panned centrally and no delays applied), the ratio is −34 dB, which, perceptually, is mono and has no width.

The musical entry that occurs immediately after this has a ratio of −4 dB, which is more typical of the long-term average of stereo signals. A way of visualising the spread of a stereo image is via what is known as a phase scope, which is now common in studio control rooms. This treats the amplitudes in the stereo signal as x and y coordinates: the right channel is plotted against the left channel, but rather than the y (left) axis being vertical and the x (right) axis being horizontal, the whole plot is rotated anticlockwise by 45 degrees. If the stereo signal has some amplitude in the right channel but zero amplitude in the left channel, then the plotted point will appear somewhere along the line of the right axis; where there is some amplitude in the left but none in the right, then the plotted point will appear somewhere along the line of the left axis. If the amplitude and the polarities are the same in the left channel (i.e. the signal is mono and in phase), then the plotted point will appear along the vertical line that is in between these two axes.

Three phase scopes showing how the stereo image changes between these three opening moments (mono voice with stereo delays; mono voice; first twelve bars from music entry) are shown in Figure 5.

The varied exploitation of the possibilities offered by the (two-channel) stereo format is an important feature of *Slave*. As Warner has also noted,

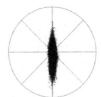 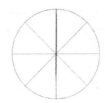 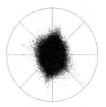

Figure 5 Phase scopes for three sections at the opening of 'Jones the Rhythm': mono spoken voice with stereo delays (left panel), mono spoken voice with no delays (middle) and first twelve bars after the music entry (right).

Slave 'makes a feature of the evocation of space or, more accurately, spaces. This sense of space is evoked in two ways: the physical position of sounds and the spatial characteristics suggested by the ambience' (Warner, 2003, p. 132). Within the opening minute of the album, this exploration of space has begun and is returned to throughout.

The music of 'Jones the Rhythm' is the original version of the song 'Slave to the Rhythm' that was intended to be the form used for the single release. As producer Trevor Horn explains, he was not satisfied with early demos of this version, originally recorded by another act (for whom the song was actually written):

> We had this song that we'd written for Frankie Goes to Hollywood called 'Slave to the Rhythm'. They'd recorded it and Holly [Johnson, lead singer of FGTH] sang it pretty well but it wasn't really them and they didn't really want to do it. Anyway, we had this very Germanic version ... almost like a very high energy dance thing and quite honestly I hated it ... The only rhythm that I, at the time, would have been prepared to be a slave to was go-go, because go-go was the most exciting thing around at that time. (Horn in Allinson and Levine, 17 April 2006)

Despite these reservations, this version was completed and recorded with Grace Jones. It is not clear exactly what Horn means by 'Germanic' in the first demo version that he heard. There is a form of this version on the 12-inch release of the single 'Slave to the Rhythm', which was released in the first week of October 1985 (Jones, 1985b). 'Annihilated Rhythm' (appearing on some releases with the alternative title 'G. I. Blues') has a tempo of 145 beats per minute (BPM) and does not feature a vocal by Jones, except for some short sampled excerpts (which do appear on *Slave*'s third track, 'Operattack').

It begins with a solo repeated electronic metronome sound with no dynamic variation, clearly stating the crotchet pulse for two bars. This then switches to a quaver rhythm that persists, again with no dynamic variation, throughout the piece. At the point that it switches to quavers, it is joined by a kick and snare drum pattern, which is also very simple in terms of note placement and (lack of) dynamic variation. The lead instrument is a sampled electric guitar that is very straightforwardly transposed to different notes, again without any variation in duration or dynamic. There is a spoken exchange 30 seconds in that mockingly questions the quality of the music:

> Questioner (unknown voice): Steve, do you think this is the worst B-side that you and Trevor have ever made?
> Steve Lipson: No [laughs]
> Questioner: Aren't you ashamed of it?
> Steve Lipson (camply): No!

The musical material is certainly limited: harmonically there is an alternation between chords I and V, with ambiguity as to whether the tonality is major or minor due to both the minor and major thirds being played by a chromatically moving quaver bassline, which characterises both the verse and the chorus; the bridge is essentially on chord II. The term 'bridge' is used in this analysis to describe a passage of music that appears between the verse and chorus of a song. This is different to the US usage of this term, which implies what is referred to in the UK as a 'middle eight', which is typically only heard once (Tagg, n.d.). 'Annihilated Rhythm' does have a middle eight that varies the rhythmic arrangement (in particular the kick drum part becomes busier), introduces new, short samples and is followed by a repeat of the bridge. Finally, towards the end of the piece, the full sung phrase 'slave to the rhythm' by Jones is heard. The piece ends on a Ic (a second inversion chordal harmony of the tonic, clearly major this time) to V (minor) progression played with a strident brass pad.

It is likely that this version is closest to the original demo by Woolley and Darlow that Horn heard, but there was also a version that FGTH worked on.

> I wrote the original track to [a] brief with Simon Darlow and The Frankies worked on it for a couple of weeks – but then gave up ... Grace recorded the vocal ... However the track at that point was the same vibe as our original demo – very square – very white ... it was almost like a Gary Glitter song! (Woolley in Walters, 2015a)

The FGTH version, completed in July 1984, exists in the ZTT audio archive (as a compact cassette, at least[8]) but has not been officially released (Harrison, 2010). Audio that purports to be this demo has appeared online (Renevolution, 2019),

---

[8] Cassette was a common way of quickly making convenient listening copies available during studio sessions, and this was sometimes done even when it was not deemed necessary to make a professional-quality master recording (e.g. to ½" inch analogue tape or DASH) at that particular stage of a session.

and it is certainly plausible as a 1984 demo version of this song with lead vocals by Holly Johnson (singer with FGTH). Here the rhythm arrangement is syncopated and sparser. For example, the kick drum is still heard on beats 1 and 3, but is augmented by a second low drum sound that has a less abrupt attack. Overall, the rhythmic arrangement is characterised by sounds that are pulled behind the beat.

As it finally appears on *Slave*, 'Jones the Rhythm' is slower, at 135 BPM, than 'Annihilated Rhythm' and the purported Frankie Goes to Hollywood demo (142), still characterised by the straight (i.e. un-swung) quavers groove of 'Annihilated Rhythm' but now combining a large orchestra and chorus (in some ways approaching Romantic opera proportions) with a small rock combo (drums, electric bass, acoustic guitar, synthesiser). The bassline of 'Annihilated Rhythm' is retained but here is replaced (or, at least, doubled) by an electric bass guitar that is able to offer a broader dynamic range and variety of articulation.

It is certainly relentless, and Jones gives a dramatic (or camp), if un-virtuosic, performance: she is singing in her lower register, but also growling and shouting. Her lead vocal is relatively lacking in reverberation compared to her background vocalisations. The reverberation does not always sound as if it is acoustically plausible. For example, her backing vocal 'I'll never, never' at 3.28 has the temporal characteristic of the AMS RMX-16 reverberator's non-linear programs, which breaks the sense of causality of natural reverberation and gives the impression that the direct sound of her voice is coalescing from the reverberation, rather than the reverberation being caused by the direct sound of her voice.

There are some aspects of the final result that are only possible with individual mic'ing and tracking of instruments. For example, the acoustic guitar can be clearly heard above other elements of the track, the possibility of which would be unlikely with all the instruments in the same room being recorded by just one or two microphones. For a pop record it is the sheer scale of the orchestra that is most unusual about this opening piece. It is a pop song and a pop production, but there is the sense of scale and drama of a grand opera. The close, individual mic'ing of a large array of acoustic instruments is also typical of the orchestral score of a large-budget Hollywood film.

The music starts with the figuration (simplified from the recording) shown in Figure 6. This figuration is also heard in the purported FGTH version but is missing from 'Annihilated Rhythm'. It is played across two bars, but it is two groups of three quavers, followed by two sets of crotchet-plus-two-quavers, all delayed by a quaver, which creates syncopation. The compass of each of the four groups of three notes is a fourth, all of them perfect except for the third group, which is augmented – essentially a sequence that moves downwards by

Figure 6 Opening motif, with simplified harmony, of 'Jones the Rhythm'.

a tone each time it is heard before finally falling a minor third. The implied harmony is a fourth below this, and so the last group of the harmony is at the same pitch (albeit an octave lower) as the first upper group.

At the beginning of the track this motif is heard four times (giving eight bars): first over Eb, then F, then Db and finally Ab. There are then four bars where Jones' voice is heard, layered and sampled, intoning the word 'slave' with a downward portamento, a motif that is also heard at the end of the piece and elsewhere on the album. At this point, the musical material from 'Annihilated Rhythm' first appears with the identical straight quaver pattern of parallel fourths (F and Bb shifting to Bb and Eb) but with subtle continuous timbral variation imparted by the use of a resonant filter whose centre frequency shifts as the pattern is being played.

Figure 7 shows a chromagram of the whole piece (not including the spoken introduction). A chromagram reassigns the energy found in each frequency channel (of which there may be many thousands if the analysed signal is minutes long) of a Fourier frequency analysis into twelve channels, representing the total energy in each of the pitch classes in the twelve-tone equal-tempered scale (Lartillot et al., 2007). The magnitude (vertical axis) is the square root of the total energy and is a measure of the average amplitude of the signal at these pitches. Pitch 'height', or octave number, is ignored so all the energy for a single chroma, or pitch class, from all of its octave shifts is captured in a single measure. The magnitude is normalised, meaning that its peak value is set to one and all other values are scaled accordingly. Although the piece is in Eb, it is interesting that the most energy is centred on the pitch of F during the piece. This is likely because of the weight that is given to this pitch during the bridge between verse and chorus, because it coincides with the third harmonic of the dominant (Bb) and its prominence in the quaver pattern of parallel fourths.

The ending of this first track is also remarkable. In fact, the song does not really end; it seems to disintegrate in the way that a particular passage might do in a rehearsal, or in a recording take that is abandoned due to a mistake. All of a sudden, this grand display presented to our ears is revealed to be just a production, a show, and we can now see (or rather hear) the machinery behind the scenes. Someone (it sounds like Horn) from the studio control room tries to

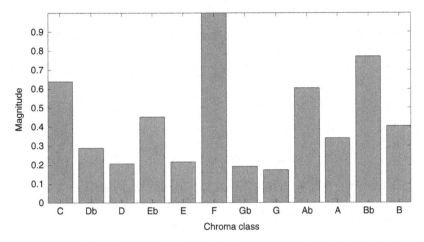

Figure 7 Pitch chromagram of 'Jones the Rhythm', generated using the Music Information Retrieval toolbox of Lartillot et al.

interrupt the singer by calling 'Grace! Grace!' via the studio talkback system; pulled out of her performance reverie, she responds 'oh, that's weird' and begins to laugh. As she laughs, we can hear howl round/feedback almost beginning to occur between her microphone and the talkback. Not only are we listening to the record, but we are listening to the record being made. A typical Horn/ZTT gesture, but it is still very rare for any recording (pop, rock or classical) to take such an approach, and the effect is quite striking.

3.2 The Fashion Show

Following the tearing down of the stage set of the opening spectacle of 'Jones the Rhythm', there is an immediate segue, without the silent pause of two or three seconds that typically demarcates album tracks, into 'The Fashion Show'. The key is now Ab, so the previous tonic now becomes the dominant. The chromagram for this track is shown in Figure 8, showing Eb (the dominant, but also the third harmonic of the tonic) as the most prominent pitch class.

The opening harmonic structure cycles between these two chords: Abm11, with the third and ninth omitted, and Ebm7, also without the third. This harmony is outlined by the bass guitar and an electric piano, or rather a digital emulation via FM synthesis of an electric piano. In her thesis on analysis of timbre, Megan Lavengood devotes an entire section to a discussion of the 'E. PIANO 1' preset sound of the Yamaha DX-7, as an example of the opposition of digital clarity to the perceived warmth of analogue synthesisers.

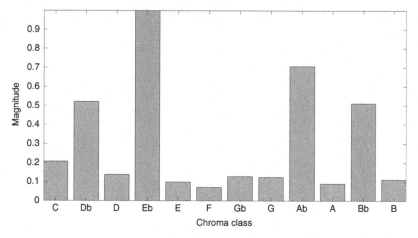

Figure 8 Pitch chromagram of 'The Fashion Show'.

E. PIANO 1, the sound of which somewhat resembled a Fender Rhodes electric piano, was one of the most-used presets of the Yamaha DX7; the preset is a paragon of the '80s sound. Essential timbral aspects of the '80s sound are encapsulated within the timbre of E. PIANO 1 – namely, brightness and clarity, two qualities that were considered particularly emblematic of digitally-synthesized sounds among musicians of the 1980s. (Lavengood, 2017, p. 104)

The DX-7 electric sound did resemble the Fender Rhodes electromechanical instrument this particular preset patch was presumably intended to emulate. In fact, the demise of the Rhodes as a viable product in the mid-1980s has been ascribed to the fact that, since the DX-7 was much lighter (because it was an entirely electronic, rather than partly mechanical, sound generator) and offered a plausible electric piano sound, it was a much more attractive instrument for gigging keyboard players. Rhodes closed its factory in 1985, two years after the launch of the DX-7 and the year that *Slave* was released (Lenhoff and Robertson, 2019, pp. 239–40). Although it resembles an electric piano sound, it does have its own distinctive timbre.

As Lavengood observes, and as shown in Figure 9, there are two sets of upper harmonics in this DX-7 patch, in addition to the first set of nine. These offer brightness but, because they are relatively sparse, the overall sound is not excessively bright or abrasive. This is one of three properties of the sound that give it its character, in addition to the harmonics being just that, integer multiples of the fundamental frequency, whereas some of the components of the Rhodes' spectrum are inharmonic. This strong harmonicity can give a sense of clarity, although it might also be heard as clinical and static (since the beating

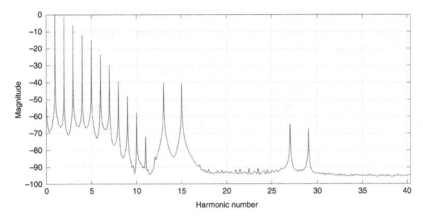

Figure 9 Spectrum of DX-7 'E. PIANO 1' patch, note C5.[9]

effects due to inharmonic partials will be absent). This irregular spacing and shaping of partials is straightforward with FM synthesis, but difficult (if not impossible) to achieve with analogue subtractive synthesis.

FM can create a vast number of sinusoids at different frequencies from just two oscillators, the carrier and the modulator (which controls the frequency of the carrier, hence the term frequency modulation), albeit in a fixed pattern whose spread can be controlled by the amplitude of the modulator. The DX-7 offered six oscillators ('operators' in Yamaha parlance) that could be configured into one of thirty-two different algorithms (essentially routings between the oscillators). Algorithm six organises the oscillators into three parallel FM pairs (containing a modulator and a carrier each), enabling three patterns of multiple partials to be included in the spectrum of the same output sound.

This sound is heard at the very beginning of the track, before giving way briefly in the fourth bar to a pad (the generic name given to a synthesised sustained sound), which has its own strong sonic identity. This sound plays a prominent role in the final track of *Slave* and was designed and created by session keyboard player Andy Richards using his Fairlight CMI. It was based on a sample of the session vocalist Carol Kenyon singing the words 'show me' and had been used in a number of well-known records, including at least two

---

[9] This sample was obtained from https://freewavesamples.com/yamaha-dx7-e-piano-1-c5. It should be noted that this spectrum of this patch is sensitive to the velocity with which the key is struck – faster velocities yield relatively more energy in the upper harmonics than lower velocities. The sampling rate of the audio is 44.1 kHz and the spectrum is created from Fourier analysis of the poles generated by an LPC analysis with order 500. LPC (linear predictive coding) is a parametric spectral estimation method and is used here because it offers a clearer depiction of the spectrum than that available by direct use of the Fourier transform on the signal itself.

others by the Horn/ZTT team that Richards played on, 'Welcome to the Pleasure Dome' by Frankie Goes to Hollywood (1984) and 'The Murder of Love' by Propaganda (1985). Sampling technology, even for just a few seconds of grainy quality that the reduced bandwidth of the Fairlight afforded, was new and hugely expensive but offered the opportunity to create and shape their very own sounds from scratch, creating distinctive sonic signatures for those players and programmers who were able to access, learn and negotiate the technology.

Another distinctive sonic signature that permeates much of *Slave* is go-go. This track is the first time that the go-go groove is heard. Tagg describes groove as:

> [The] sense of gross-motoric movement produced by one or more simultan-
> eously sounded rhythmic-metric-timbral-tonal patterns lasting, as single
> units, no longer than the extended present ['a duration roughly equivalent
> to no more than that of a musical phrase (inhalation + exhalation or long
> exhalation), or to a few footsteps'], and repeated throughout a musical
> episode or piece. Groove can also denote other types of perceived gross-
> motoric movement, as in work songs and marches. (Tagg, n.d.)

Timbre is as much a part of groove as rhythm is. This can be easily verified by imagining a typical kick drum and hi hat pattern and swapping the instruments, so that the kick now plays the hi hat part and vice versa: clearly the groove is significantly altered, even though the division of time is the same. Timbre is a slippery concept (e.g. Siedenburg and McAdams, 2017) but here it is considered as a perceptual attribute that corresponds strongly with the physical sound properties of spectrum and temporal envelope, that is, a sound's spectrum and how it changes over time.

As has already been discussed, the arrival of new technologies in the time immediately preceding *Slave* enabled increasingly precise editing of both the temporal and spectral qualities of sound elements as well as tools to capture (sample) small components and precisely arrange (sequence) them (and within exact, metronomic grids, if desired). That is not to say that the new technologies enabled groove to become a part of music. In fact, some (e.g. Beato, 2019) might say that the metronomic quantisation that the tools enabled mitigated *against* groove or at least rigidly fixed one of its expressive features. Groove does not need machines to exist and likely existed in some of the earliest music. But the new technologies did enable groove to be mediated post hoc to a far greater extent. 'Metronomic' is one type of groove, just as other types may exist that are partly characterised by malleability of pulse.

Danielson describes how the repetitive nature of groove can draw listeners (and for 'listeners', read also 'dancers', 'workers', 'athletes' etc.) into music to the extent that their movement and perception of time become enmeshed within it:

> In groove-oriented music, the basic unit of the song is repeated so many times that our inclination as listeners to organize the musical material into an overall form gradually fades away. Instead of waiting for events to come, we are submerged in what is before us. Our focus turns inward, as if our sensibility for details, for timing inflections and tiny timbral nuances, is inversely proportional to musical variation on a larger scale … We operate within a continuous field where the limit between music and listener is not yet established or has vanished. Dancing, playing, and listening in such a state of being are not characterized by consideration or reflection but rather by a presence in the here and now of the event. (Danielsen, 2010)

Go-go is a scene and a style of music that emerged as an intersection of hip-hop and funk in Washington, DC, in the late seventies. The go-go groove is a 'rhythmic pattern created by the interaction of the drums, congas and roto-toms' (Lornell and Stephenson, 2009, p. ix). Here it is at a medium tempo (97 BPM), swung and with a strong sense of groups of two crotchets in the bar, falling heavily on the first beat of each. Rather than performed entirely live, as was often the case with go-go, what is heard here is a combination of sampled rhythms (captured from players recorded specifically for the production) and those constructed by sequencing individual samples or syntheses of instruments, such as the clap/snare hybrid that appears on the second beat of each bar.

The rhythm and tempo work well as an evocation of the catwalk: the metrical division into two-beat units matching the bipedal motion and a striding pace carrying a sonically sophisticated update of a relatively new and fashionable American musical culture.

To capture this sound, the production team travelled to New York to record established go-go musicians in the city, but Horn found them atypical of session musicians that he was used to working with:

> We had a band of really great Go-go musicians: some people from Experience Unlimited, some from Trouble Funk … and they could all really play – but nobody could remember an arrangement. In fact, they were baffled by the idea of an arrangement. They just started, kept going and then they stopped. And they'd all play together all the way through, with all instruments leaking into the drum microphones. (Horn in Lindvall, 2012)

With a meticulous approach to capturing and shaping sound such as Horn's, leakage is to be avoided where possible since it prevents isolated, individual instruments and performances being available separately on different tracks. Without good separation, choices at the mixing stage, such as relative levels between parts and their temporal and spectral shape, are constrained, which would be anathema to Horn. This situation frustrated the recording process until, as Lipson explained, a lucky accident occurred:

> The guitar player went to the loo at one point. He was away for about two minutes and [for] those two minutes we had drums without guitar on them. It was fortuitous, really ... Listened through the multitrack, found the two minutes of rhythm without any guitar, went back to Trevor's hotel room and rewrote the song. Then, went the next day back to the studio (very expensive, money *pouring* out), I copied the rhythm and, I think we were there for five days in all so we must have spent two or three days ... doing nothing but editing the drums to this song that only just existed and we were formatting the song as I was editing the drums. (Lipson in Allison and Levine, 2006)

The substantial amount of editing implies that it was not just leakage that was a challenge in terms of fitting go-go to this production style. Musicians who play live will often vary in tempo, even if it is not significant enough to be immediately recognisable as such by a listener. Tempo variation can be a feature of groove. For example, the players may naturally slow down slightly as they vary their patterns to create what is known as a fill at the end of a four or eight bar phrase. To get an idea of how this feature of a typical go-go groove of that time compares with that of 'The Fashion Show', it is instructive to see how their tempi vary.

Figure 10 provides a comparison between the tempo of the middle three minutes of 'The Fashion Show' (solid black line) and the middle three minutes of the vocal mix of the band E.U.'s track 'E.U. Freeze' (E.U., 1985) (solid grey line), released in the same year as *Slave* and so likely recorded at a similar time. They have slightly different mean tempi ('E.U. Freeze' is about 103 BPM, still within the broad range of go-go), but the remarkable difference is in the variation in tempo of 'E. U. Freeze' compared to the constancy of 'The Fashion Show'. This precisely illustrates the difference between the Horn- and Lipson-produced and technologised go-go groove that appears on much of *Slave* (with the exception of 'Ladies and Gentlemen: Miss Grace Jones', discussed later in this section), and the one that is captured live in 'Freeze'. It is subjugated and contained within an utterly consistent pulse (rhythm as the song's manacle); this contradicts one of its core characteristics, as stated by Lornell and Stephenson, that it 'thrives in live performances' (Lornell and Stephenson, 2009, p. ix). Yet this consistency affords augmentation of timbre (and therefore groove) via the precise layering of sound (such as the hybrid clap/snare mentioned earlier) using the sequencing tools at their disposal. The track 'Junkyard', which, along with 'Annihilated Rhythm', appeared on the 12"

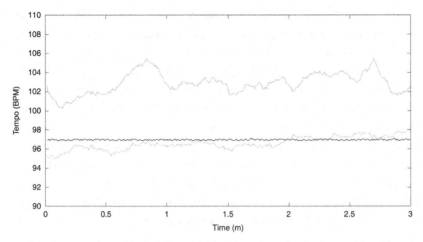

Figure 10 Tempo profiles of the middle three minutes of 'The Fashion Show' (solid black line), 'Freeze' (solid grey line) and 'Junk Yard' (dotted grey line).[11]

single release of 'Slave', offers an intriguing halfway house between the entirely live groove of 'Freeze' and the constant tempo of 'Fashion'. The tempo of the middle three minutes of this track is shown as a dotted line in Figure 10. There are recognisable sonic elements from the final *Slave* production (such as the snare fill, which is heard in isolation on the final track, named 'Ladies and Gentlemen: Miss Grace Jones' but released as the single 'Slave to Rhythm'), and there are interventions in the mixing (such as a significant amount of reverberation applied to occasional snare strikes, whereas the majority are heard relatively dry), but the tempo varies over a range of about three BPM and so the material has not yet been fully conformed to the metronomic grid of 'The Fashion Show'. The title could be a self-deprecating indication of the status of the material: scrap, yet to be sifted and sculpted into the final production (and this would fit with the title of 'Annihilated Rhythm' as the description of a non-groove). It may also be a tribute to The Junkyard Band, a group that initially formed as children, living on the Barry Farms housing projects in Washington, DC, in 1980 playing go-go on found objects such as plastic buckets and drink cans. They were signed by Def Jam records and released 'Sardines' in 1985, the year of *Slave*'s release.[10]

---

[11] These data were obtained via the QMUL beat tracker plugin in Sonic Visualiser, exported to Matlab and smoothed with a 16-beat (four bar) moving average filter. The micro variations seen in the tempo derived from 'Fashion' are likely due to small errors in the pulse position estimation caused by variations in the instrumentation during the track, rather than changes in the tempo of the audio itself.

[10] www.junkyardband.us/.

Throughout the piece, fragments of the lyrics are heard sung by both Jones and then by the backing singer Tessa Niles, with her voice transitioning from left to right as she repeats 'to the rhythm' towards the end. There is a distinct contrast in the singing styles and vocal timbres. Whereas Jones is dramatic and characterful yet demonstrates limited technique, Niles is more technically accomplished yet bland (which is arguably the right combination for a backing singer who supports and embellishes, but does not overshadow, the lead performance). Even those associated with her accept that Jones' singing technique is limited. Jean-Paul Goude, who collaborated with her extensively in designing her costumes and directing her stage shows, as well as photographing and painting her for much of her album artwork, and with whom she had a child, makes the following observation in his autobiography:

> Personally, I always loved Grace's voice, flaws included, especially when she'd become dramatic. But if one wished to be picky, she was an easy target. She had been singing for less than two years [in the late seventies] and wasn't an accomplished vocalist. But she had something much more important. She offered a whole new sensibility which was far more interesting to me than just an ability to sing properly. (Goude, 1981, p. 103)

Bruce Woolley has commented on the delivery of her performance for the record:

> Grace is amazing in the studio – when she's 'On' that is . . . some singers really need to be coaxed onto the microphone and a lot of the recording process is taken up with working up to that moment. (Trevor [Horn] is a master of this btw) Grace is one of these singers – but once she's in the zone, it's like three or four takes – and you can't tell her what to do; her timing is incredible – you can't analyse it – it doesn't make sense – you can shift her voice and try to correct it – but it won't be as good . . . in my experience anyway. (Walters, 2015a)

Both of these observations are reminders of Penman's words heard at the beginning of the record: 'What do you still want from me?' says the singer . . . 'Exact presence that no fantasy can represent.'

3.3 Operattack

This piece is constructed entirely from samples of the voice recordings of Jones and Ian McShane. Whereas all of the other tracks maintain a strict pulse (all of them are based on samples – individual percussive sounds and/or short loops of played drums and percussion – which are then computer sequenced), here the tempo is very elastic, a loosening of the rhythmic shackles to which the music has been enslaved so far.

The samples are often played at different speeds to those at which they were recorded: this has the effect of slowing down or speeding up the sounds but also changing their pitch. These pitch and time distortions are quite obvious and cartoonish: the digital tools for more subtly and flexibly manipulating the voice that are now commonplace were not available in either the Fairlight or Synclavier and more advanced and elaborate tools for the manipulation of digital audio were at that time confined to the mainframe computers of research establishments such as the Institut de Recherche et Coordination Acoustique/ Musique (IRCAM) in Paris. However, the tools used here do effect an interesting ambiguity at times in the separate identities of Jones and McShane, and the more subtle alterations also evoke gender and age shifts. The acoustic parallel of a recording being slowed down, and therefore extending in duration and falling in pitch, is that the source of the sound (real or imagined) appears to get larger, and the opposite occurs for a sound that is sped up.

This track also continues the exploration of the spatial 'left/right axis' (Warner, 2003, p. 133). At the time of *Slave*'s issue, the presentation of sounds within and between the two channels of stereo had been largely settled in an orthodoxy that emerged in the early 1970s and continues to this day: the lead vocal and instruments with predominantly low-frequency energy presented in the centre of the image (i.e. arriving at the same time and with the same energy from both loudspeakers), with other instruments, and reverberation, surrounding them in the image in a balanced (although not strictly symmetric) way.

Prior to this orthodoxy, a disparity of sonic placement is observed in productions of the 1960s. For example, the placement of many sounds solely in either one speaker or the other (Dockwray and Moore, 2010). The universal tool for placing a sound within the ('phantom', since there are no loudspeakers at the position from which sound appears to be arriving) image between two loudspeakers is a panoramic potentiometer ('pan pot' for short), a device for adjusting the level of a sound in the left and right channels in a complementary way: moving the control to the right increases the signal level in the right channel and reduces it in the left channel, causing, for those properly situated in the stereo 'sweet spot' equidistant between the two loudspeakers, the phantom source of the sound to move away from the left to the right loudspeaker.

A problem with stereo delivered via two loudspeakers is that the sweet spot is very small. As soon as the listener's position shifts from the centre, then sound arrives at them earlier from one loudspeaker than it does from the other. A very strong cue for locating the source of a sound is the direction from which the sound arrives first, so as soon as one loudspeaker becomes closer than the other and sound arrives from it even just a few milliseconds earlier, all sounds appear to be emanating from that loudspeaker, even though both loudspeakers are contributing to the overall sound that is heard. The only time that sounds will be perceived as emanating from the same place, no matter where the listener, is if they come solely from one loudspeaker or the other. Therefore, although mixes from the early era of stereo that have individual instruments and voices in either the left or the right loudspeaker but not both may sound primitive and unnatural, they do at least have the advantage that the placement of sounds is the same for anyone regardless of where they are in the room.

Although the album explores a number of uses of two-channel stereo, nearly all of the sound placements in 'Operattack', except for reverberation, are in either one channel or the other. It combines cacophony with antiphony: the presentation of sounds in a seemingly chaotic spatial and temporal order at times (such as the opening half-minute) with ordered (turn-taking) statements and responses, which are spatially organised with a clear temporal scheme characterised by a regular alternation between channels and periods of signifi-cant accelerandi that are the opposite of the immutable tempi of other pieces. The exploration of antiphony is possibly an exaggerated allusion to the 'call and response' of African American forms including go-go, something that is absent from the groove-based evocations of this genre elsewhere on the record.

Another spatial element that is explored here is reverberation: some of the sounds are heard completely 'dry' (i.e. without any reverberation, anechoic); others are heard 'wet'. The reverberation of a room is that part of its response to sound where energy is arriving randomly from all directions. This is an ideal that well-designed auditoria can get close to, and it manifests itself as signals arriving at each ear that have the same character (i.e. are both due to the response of the same room) but are decorrelated from each other; this is something that humans find immersive and satisfying (Schroeder, 1979). In this case, provided the reverberation presented by one loudspeaker is decorre-lated from that presented by the other, this immersive 'binaural dissimilarity' will persist even if the listener is not in the sweet spot. Here then, where sounds are reverberated, regardless of which channel the (direct) sound is heard in, its reverberation is heard, decorrelated, in both channels. So the form of stereo presentation adopted for this piece preserves spatial antiphony whilst retaining a distinct spatial feature of natural reverberation. 'Staging' of the voice has been an important part of pop production since at least Elvis Presley's work (dis-cussed in the previous section) and has been the subject of much study, for example Lacasse (2000) and Dockwray and Moore (2010). The variety of staging of the voice (both Jones' and McShane's) throughout *Slave* is unusually broad, particularly in this movement.

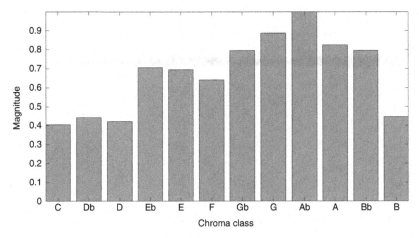

Figure 11 Chromagram for 'Operattack'.

Although much of the material does not elicit a strong sense of pitch (because it is spoken, of short duration or is a noisy sound such as breath), it is instructive to see how energy is distributed in the chromagram shown in Figure 11. As expected, there is a much more even distribution of energy across the twelve chromas, although, interestingly, the most energy is at A flat and its octaves, which is the tonic of the previous piece and the subdominant of the opening.

Structurally, the piece can be crudely divided into three sections: cacophony (a 13-second presentation of a number of utterances heard together with varying start times, pitches and left or right position with no readily apparent scheme, followed by a repeat), antiphony (approximately a minute and a half of utterances, usually heard answering each other between channels, that begins and ends with accelerandi) and, finally, cacophony (21 seconds in duration ending with a ritardando).

The effect of the cacophony is impressive, but it is bewildering and difficult to deconstruct. A very useful tool for its analysis is correlation. Recall from the previous section that cross-correlation is a measure of the similarity between two different signals. At a shift where there is a very strong similarity, then that suggests that at this point one of the signals contains the other.

In the analysis that follows, the use of common material between the cacophonous and antiphonal sections is demonstrated using cross-correlation. Individual utterances are captured from the central section where they are heard in isolation and then their cross-correlation with each channel of the whole piece is calculated. It is worthwhile recalling the similarity between digital delays and sampling that was mentioned in the previous section: both techniques capture digital audio

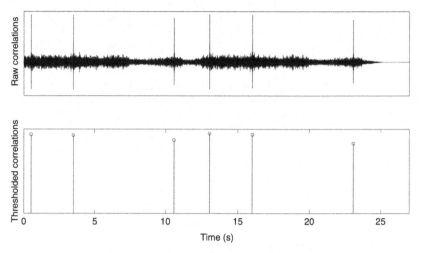

Figure 12 The derivation of sample start positions via cross-correlation of one short excerpt ('work to the rhythm', heard in the left channel at 43 seconds) with the left channel of the first section of 'Operattack' (27 seconds).

samples in memory for later playback. That playback is determined by a pause of a specified duration in a delay processor, and a trigger (such as the keyboard of a Fairlight or Synclavier) in a sampler.

The process is demonstrated in Figure 12. The top panel shows the outcome of shifting a short mono sample (in the sense of a short digital recording of a sound) of the utterance 'work to the rhythm' taken from the middle section of the piece (in the left channel at 0.43), against the left channel of the whole piece, one sample (in the sense of a single instant of capture in a digital audio signal) at a time, and measuring the correlation between the two at each of those shifts. Very strong localised peaks can be observed, and it is very likely that these are because the piece contains this sample at this pitch at these precise times. The lower panel shows the result of thresholding this correlation output, so that just the likely onset points of the sample can be seen.

If the sample occurs in the piece at different pitches to that of the isolated example, then this process will not detect those occurrences. To identify these, the sample is pitch shifted and the correlation and thresholding process is repeated for each of these shifts. Figure 13 shows the thresholded locations for each of the pitch shifts (denoted by different colour stems) for both channels (top and middle panels). To illustrate the relationship with the actual audio of this section of the piece, its audio is shown in the bottom panel.

To show how material is combined throughout this piece, the audio of the opening is now analysed in detail. Warner identifies four spoken phrases that are

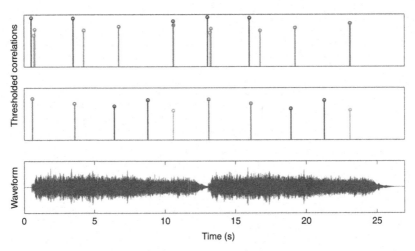

Figure 13 Markers indicating the position (horizontal) and strength (vertical) of correlations between the same utterance as Figure 12 and the left (top) and right (middle) channels of the opening section of 'Operattack'. The correlations occur at the same pitch (blue), a whole tone lower (orange), a minor third lower (yellow) and a perfect fourth lower (mauve). The audio waveform is also shown (bottom, left channel: turquoise; right channel: green).

used in this section: three spoken by Jones and one by McShane (Warner, 2003, p. 130). The previous and following figures show the thresholded correlations for instances of these utterances where they appear in isolation against the opening section of the piece: 'work to the rhythm' (Figures 12 and 13), 'annihilating the rhythm' (Figure 14), 'dance to the rhythm' (Figure 15) and 'slave to the rhythm' (Figure 16). The correlation with the utterance of the single word 'slave' with sinking pitch is also presented in Figure 17, since this sample is a prominent element throughout the album (it is first heard just after the spoken introduction to 'Jones the Rhythm'). Each sample has been pitch shifted to identify where strong correlations occur, and these are shown as different coloured stems (as in Figure 13).

We can observe a number of things in these plots that are difficult to discern by listening alone. The repetition of the first half of the section in the second half can be clearly seen in the positions of the sample onsets. The impression of a group of voices is created by triggering samples at slightly different pitches at the same time: these slight differences in pitch also cause slight differences in length of the samples and therefore the timing of different words within them. Differences in how phrases are distributed can also be seen. For example, samples of 'dance to the rhythm' occur nearer the start of each section, whereas 'annihilating the rhythm' appears towards the end of them.

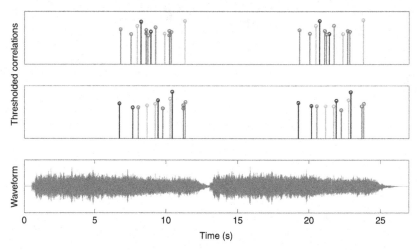

Figure 14 Markers indicating the position of correlations between the utterance 'annihilating the rhythm' (heard at 48 seconds in the right channel) and the left (top) and right (middle) channels of the opening section of 'Operattack'. The correlations occur at the same pitch (blue), a whole tone higher (orange), a minor third higher (yellow) and a perfect fourth higher (mauve). The audio waveform is also shown (bottom, left channel: turquoise; right channel: green).

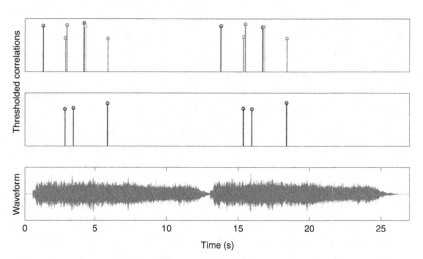

Figure 15 Markers indicating the position of correlations between the utterance 'dance to the rhythm' (heard at one minute and 11 seconds in the right channel) and the left (top) and right (middle) channels of the opening section of 'Operattack'. The correlations occur at the same pitch (blue), a semitone lower (orange), a whole tone lower (yellow), a minor third lower (mauve) and a perfect fourth lower (dark green). The audio waveform is also shown (bottom, left channel: turquoise; right channel: green).

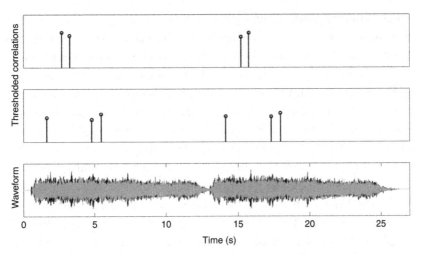

Figure 16 Markers indicating the position correlations between the utterance 'slave to the rhythm' (heard at 58 seconds in the left channel) and the left (top) and right (middle) channels of the opening section of 'Operattack'. The correlations occur at the same pitch (there are no transpositions). The audio waveform is also shown (bottom, left channel: black; right channel: grey).

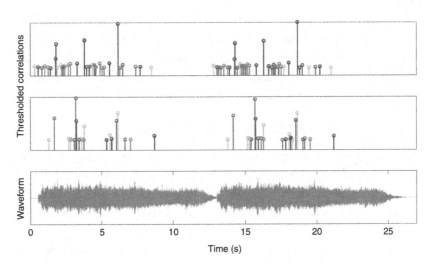

Figure 17 Markers indicating the position correlations between the utterance 'slave', gradually sinking in pitch (heard at 43 seconds in the right channel) and the left (top) and right (middle) channels of the opening section of 'Operattack'. The correlations occur at six different pitches ranging from one tone above to a minor third below the original pitch. The audio waveform is also shown (bottom, left channel: turquoise right channel: green

Steve Lipson is credited, amongst other things, with 'synclavier program-ming' on *Slave* and has said 'I did nearly the whole album on the Synclavier' (Tingen, 1987, p. 55). This is a piece that is likely to have been assembled entirely using this instrument. The full bandwidth of the audio sampling of the Synclavier is evident: throughout the piece there is energy present right across the full range of the audible spectrum. Where the Fairlight does appear on *Slave* it seems to be more band-limited. For example, the 'show me' pad of Andy Richards, first heard in the opening (0.05 to 0.10) of 'The Fashion Show', exhibits very little energy above 5 kHz. This gives that particular sound a welcome quality that many would describe as warmth, but the band-limited quality of the early models of the CMI would have likely been unsuitable for constructing an entire piece. Horn has commented that the Fairlight 'used to do this funny thing where it took all the top frequencies and all the bottom frequencies off the sample and it sort of romanticised the sound, a little bit like black and white does to a picture' (Horn in Niles, 2009). Here the Synclavier is much more transparent in its presentation of sound and the audible quality of its constituent components is retained. The available memory is likely to have constrained how much material could have been assembled, forcing Lipson to be economic with what he selected.

The fact that McShane's voice is amongst the material indicates that this piece was not completed until very close to the release of the album. Looking at how the audio is arranged, there is a sense that this is an improvisation, or a collage assembled quite randomly at first, before being ordered and refined by the sequencing and editing features of the Synclavier.

3.4 SLAVE TO THE RHYTHM

The capitalisation of this track occurs on the sleeves/covers/inlays of all ver-sions of this record, so it is clearly deliberate. It is also something of a red herring, since this is not the track that was released as the single 'Slave to the Rhythm' (that is 'Ladies and Gentleman: Miss Grace Jones', which appears later).

There is a return to elements of the go-go groove (with the same tempo) but changes in instrumentation and a sparser bass part make the opening and closing sections of this piece an interesting hybrid between the first two on the album: the drama of the first, evoked with the alternation between bold unison state-ments of Ab (I) and Eb (V), and the tempo and syncopation of the second. Ab and Eb are the most dominant pitches in the chromagram for this piece, shown in Figure 18.

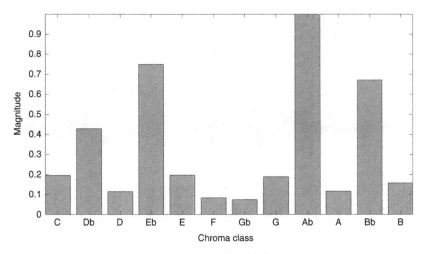

Figure 18 Chromagram for 'SLAVE TO THE RHYTHM'.

The middle section (of 16 bars with a two-bar tag to make a total of 18) begins with a shift to Gb in the bass, followed by Eb, Bb and Ab. Rhythmically it switches from the relatively sparse but highly syncopated cowbell-like sound that has been the prominent signifier of the go-go groove so far, to a triangle part with a swung-semiquaver feel. The strident hybrid snare sound is replaced with finger snaps that vary subtly in timbre. In both sections more elaborate kick drum patterns are heard, with a nuance of timing and timbre that suggest live playing, which are in contrast to the sparser patterns in 'The Fashion Show'.

During the closing section the arrangement breaks down to just drums and other percussion, a confusion of shouted vocals (in the same way as some of the backing vocals for 'Jones the Rhythm', a non-linear reverberation seems to have been applied) and occasional utterances (e.g. 'keep it up' from Jones). The kick drum is fairly high in the mix at this point and its pattern can be readily discerned. Figure 19 shows a single bar from this section, over a demisemiquaver grid with kick and snare onsets marked with an arrow. The snare placements are exactly on the second and fourth beats, but the kick drum placement is more elastic. The groove is swung, so not every subdivision of the pulse will fall evenly on a demisemiquaver grid, but in these moments between snare strikes the kick is on (particularly where it coincides with the pulse, or quaver divisions of it), slightly ahead of or slightly behind the grid and a triplet feel is apparent just before the snare on the fourth beat. This kind of variation evokes the sense of go-go's 'live-ness' whilst it remains, at the level of the crotchet pulse, utterly wedded to an unwavering tempo.

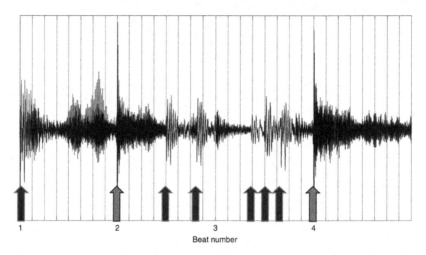

Figure 19 Mono (left mixed with right channel) waveform of the bar starting at 4.35. The kick drum (black) and snare (grey) onsets are denoted by the upwards arrows.

Material from subsequent tracks is also anticipated. At the end we are left on an Ab chord (as usual with an added fourth/eleventh, but no third) played by a synthesiser pad, which harks back to the analogue, subtractive synthesis of electronic musical instruments available before the advent of digital FM synthesis. This pad sound begins with a relatively dark timbre, but the low-pass filter applied is dynamically adjusted so that a brighter, fizzier sound emerges at the very end that is, overall, a counter to the intensity of the outer sections of this piece.

3.5 The Frog and The Princess

This is the fifth of eight tracks on the album, and it opens side two of the vinyl and cassette formats of the release. It is the only track apart from 'Jones the Rhythm', which opens side one and the whole album, to feature multiple lines of spoken word. Considering that the vinyl and cassette formats (dominant at the time, compared to CD, as discussed previously) divide albums into two distinct halves or acts, the placing of the spoken word at the start of each lends a symmetry to the program. This symmetry is not present on the alternative edition that was initially released, where this item appears on the first side, between 'The Fashion Show' and 'Operattack', with 'SLAVE TO THE RHYTHM' opening side two.

This time the text is taken from *Jungle Fever*, Jean-Paul Goude's autobiographical portfolio published in 1983, which recounts his professional and romantic relationship with Jones. It seems to be almost universally assumed that, as for 'Jones the Rhythm', it is Ian McShane that is reading the text. However, the quality of voice is quite different between the two pieces: 'Jones the Rhythm' presents an actorly baritone resonance, whereas the voice on 'Frog and Princess' is thinner timbrally – more 'narration' than 'oration' – with less resonance in the lower end of the spectrum, even though the fundamental frequency of phonation (the frequency at which the vocal folds are vibrating) is in a similar range, if a little higher.

Whereas 'Jones' is spoken word followed by music, here the words are interleaved with the music. Whilst it is feasible that the editing could have been done in time, given that McShane has said that he did his recording in the same month that the album was released, it seems unlikely that his recording also included the text for this piece, especially given the dissimilarity in the timbral quality of the recorded voices between the two. The credit that he receives on the album sleeve (for both editions) is given as 'text; extracts from I. Penman's 'The Annihilation of Rhythm' – read on the record by Ian McShane'. There is no indication that he also read the *Jungle Fever* extracts, although there is no specific credit given to anyone else. It is not Jean-Paul Goude, whose voice does appear on the longer edition (speaking at the end of 'The Fashion Show') and has a strong French accent that is not evident in the reading here. Perhaps the identity of the narrator is not revealed so that the person most strongly associated with the words is the person who wrote them: Goude.

The picture painted by the extracts is of Goude being taken in, and taken over, by Jones, but also of Jones being taken over by Goude. There is (quite possibly faux) self-deprecation in the title, with Goude cast as the ugly partner to the beautiful model, and via a derogatory term 'frog' for someone of French nationality. As 'Grace let me take her over completely' (Goude, 1981, p. 107), the sample of the single word 'slave' spoken with a sinking pitch, which appears throughout the album and is one of its most recognisable motifs, is heard.

The backdrop to this spoken text is a study in syncopation, with a tempo of 84 BPM providing space for considerable temporal variation of percussion samples. For example, imbuing sounds with a machine-like charge by sometimes truncating their reverb and then allowing the release portion of the sounds to be heard, also varying their pitch upwards to impart a sense of tension (quite literally, since when vibrating objects are put under greater tension their frequencies of vibration do increase). This timbral-rhythmic invention is built over a four-bar pentatonic ostinato, in the Dorian mode on Eb (shown in Figure 21), which is repeated throughout, with constant shifts in the instruments' assignment to it and their relative levels in the mix.

Figure 20 Ostinato figure heard throughout 'The Frog and The Princess'.

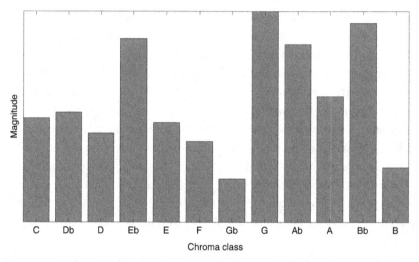

Figure 21 Chromagram for 'The Frog and The Princess'.

In the opening it is played by a combination of timbres: one typical of the sound of resonant low-pass filtered subtractive analogue synthesis, the other a thinner, brighter sound that is closer to FM synthesis. There is slow, continuous cross-fading between the two, and an octave doubling of the part also rises and falls in amplitude over time. The assigned instruments do not always exhibit a strong sense of pitch. For example, a high-pitched tom-like sound is sometimes used, and where this occurs later in the piece, the harmonies are allowed to stray from the Eb Dorian of the ostinato. For example, at the point where he mentions the painted photograph of her – 'blue black' (*Blue Black in Black on Brown* (Goude, 1981) became the cover art for her 1981 album *Nightclubbing* (Jones, 1981)) – the colour of the harmonies shifts dramatically, the lines become chromatic and angular and, at that exact point, a prominent G natural is heard. This is actually the pitch class with the most energy, as shown in the chromagram for the piece in Figure 20 and, overall, there is a broader distribution of energy across chroma that reflects the harmonically adventurous development that occurs towards the end of the piece. At the very end, the progression that is used for the harmonisation of the chorus in the final piece of the album emerges, with the G as the major third of the dominant (Eb).

3.6 The Crossing (Ooh the Action . . .)

This piece can seem rather slight. There is no lead vocal (spoken or sung), there is no dance groove and the tendency to parallel fourths on a pentatonic scale is neither adventurous nor nuanced. The predominance of the five pentatonic pitches can be seen in the chromagram (Figure 22). However, it does create a link between the pieces that precede and follow it; the first part of the ostinato figure from 'Frog and Princess' is heard, at the same pitch and the same tempo but in a new context of Gb major, which anticipates the Gb major ninth with which the following 'Don't Cry It's Only the Rhythm' opens.

Warner has noted a dynamically changing spatial presentation in this piece: 'What is unusual here is not only the change in mix between dry and reverberant sound through the track but also the extremely unnatural sound of the reverberation itself: this effect is set up in such a way as to negate any notion of the emulation of real reverberation' (Warner, 2003, p. 133). The 'unnatural sound of the reverberation' that is referred to is probably due to its bright (i.e. more energy at high frequencies than low) and very diffuse nature: it acts as a thin mist or halo around the sound and is quite different from the reverberation heard in actual enclosed spaces. The gradual bleed of sounds from distinct hard right and left positions into the centre in some way depicts 'the crossing' of the title.

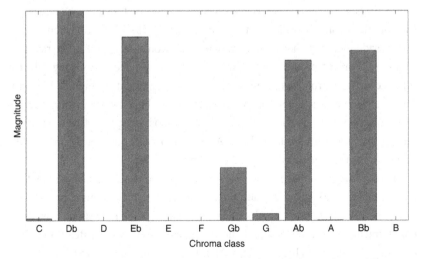

Figure 22 Chromagram for 'The Crossing (Ooh the Action . . .)'.

There is another spatial phenomenon that occurs near the beginning of this piece and is quite possibly an unintended coincidence, but is remarkable nonetheless. The phase scope was introduced earlier in this section as a way of visually representing spatial presentation of two-channel stereo. There are particular patterns that can be produced when one sine wave is fed into one channel, and another sine wave, possibly of different amplitude, frequency and starting phase, is fed into the other channel. The relationships between those three parameters for the two sine waves will determine the patterns that are seen. For example, as already discussed, if all three parameters are identical, then a vertical line will be seen. If the phases are half a wave cycle apart (i.e. the two sine waves are out of phase) but the other two parameters are the same, then a horizontal line will be seen. If the amplitude of the left channel sine wave is zero, then a line pointing in the right direction at 45 degrees will be seen, and the line will be pointing in the left direction if the right channel amplitude is zero when the left channel amplitude is non-zero. If the frequencies remain the same but there are differences in phase between the two (except for the case of being perfectly out of phase), then an elliptical shape is seen, which is a circle if the amplitudes in the two channels are identical. If there are differences in frequency, then more elaborate patterns are seen. All of these shapes and patterns are referred to as Lissajous figures and are named after the French physicist who demonstrated in the middle of the eighteenth century how they could be produced by shining a beam of light at two tuning forks with mirrors attached and positioned at right angles to each other (Greenslade, 1993).

Although sine waves are considered fundamental building blocks of sound, they are rarely heard in isolation in the natural environment or in audio productions. Real-world sounds and musical signals are typically characterised by complex combinations of these building blocks and are often 'non-stationary', meaning that their parameters are constantly, and often rapidly, changing. For one or two fleeting moments, however, the softly sung 'oh' of 'oh, the action' produces a small number of significant harmonics that are stationary for half a second or so. Somehow, in these instances the relative phase between the left and right channels is almost exactly halfway between being fully in and fully out of phase. At these moments concentric circles, 'O' shapes, appear in the phase scope, shown in Figure 23.

These three images depict, in these moments, sinusoids in each channel of approximately the same amplitude and frequency but in 'quadrature' phase with each other. Whilst quadrature processing of signals is used in areas such as radio communications, there were no audio processing devices that offered this fine control over the inter-channel phase relationships that I am aware of. It is most likely a chance occurrence, but a rather intriguing one that unwittingly depicts

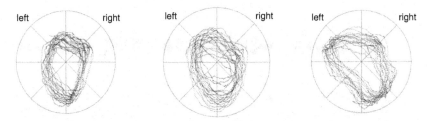

Figure 23 Phase scopes of three successive moments, totalling one quarter of a second in duration, that occur at 0.13 in 'The Crossing (Ooh the Action . . .)'.

the 'oh' being sung and predates deliberate inclusion of images in audio signals, such as by Aphex Twin in 'Equation' (1999).

3.7 Don't Cry It's Only the Rhythm

This is an exploration of material already heard in 'The Fashion Show' and 'SLAVE', with the spatial explorations of previous pieces now developed in extremis. If the difference between distinct left/right and spread spatial positioning is subtly explored elsewhere on this album, here it is brought right to the fore. The piece begins in mono with a sample of a mixed snare and cymbal being repeated as it increases in pitch. Tension is heightened by this gesture and there is a sense of tightening of some sort of machinery.

Figure 24 shows the waveform of this opening three or so seconds along with what is known as a scalogram. This is similar to the spectrogram, a visualisation tool that is used often in audio production analysis, but differs in some fundamental ways. The spectrogram is a depiction of how the distribution of energy in a signal across frequency changes over time. This is achieved by dividing the signal up into short frames, each typically somewhere between one fortieth and one twentieth of a second in duration, and performing a Fourier analysis on each. In the last three decades the Fourier transform has become a hugely important tool for both audio processing and audio analysis. It divides the spectrum up into bands that have equal width (about 40 Hz for one fortieth of a second, about 20 Hz for one twentieth of a second). This 'constant bandwidth' analysis is useful when sound components are equally spaced, such as is the case for a single instrument note containing harmonics (which are equally spaced because their frequencies are integer multiples of a fundamental frequency). However, it does not match the way in which the human auditory system senses sound, which is much closer to what is known as 'constant Q'.

With constant Q, regions of the spectrum have the same ratio of bandwidth to centre frequency. So, whereas as constant bandwidth system might have one

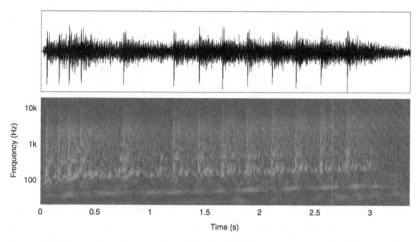

Figure 24 Time-domain waveform (top) and scalogram (bottom) of the opening of 'Don't Cry'.

region between 100 Hz and 200 Hz and another 1.0 kHz and 1.1 kHz (both have a bandwidth of 100 Hz), a constant Q system might have one region between 100 Hz and 200 Hz and another between 1 kHz and 2 kHz: although they have very different bandwidths (100 Hz and 1 kHz), the ratio between their bandwidths and their centre frequencies is the same. The spectrogram can be a very useful tool, but it tends to get used without much consideration as to whether it is the most appropriate one for the type of signal being analysed, or the sort of information being sought. On a spectrogram the distance between two frequencies an octave apart is depicted in a linear way, that is, it increases as the centre frequency between them increases (because a note that is an octave higher than another has a fundamental frequency that is double that of the lower note). But that is not how we perceive the distance between them or how they are laid out, for example, on the keyboard of a piano.

The term scalogram refers to an image that depicts how energy is distributed across different scales of the spectrum, as opposed to bands, and is constant Q. At higher frequencies the analysis bandwidths are higher than they are at lower frequencies. Because of something known as time-frequency uncertainty, which places limits on how well we can simultaneously resolve the position of energy in time *and* frequency, this also means that at higher frequencies there is more precision about where events occur in time. The scalogram is ideally suited to observing audio that is played by a sampler. This is because when a sampler plays something at a lower pitch, it also plays it for a longer time (think about a tape recording of speech slowing down: not only does the pitch get lower but its duration increases, too). When this simultaneous scaling of pitch and time is happening, then identical motifs will appear with different heights (pitch) and lengths (duration) but the observed visual pattern of the motif will be the same, just presented at a different scale.

The upper panel of Figure 24 shows the waveform of the opening three seconds of 'Don't Cry'. The onsets of the sample repetitions can be seen, but little else can be discerned from the waveform. The lower panel shows a scalogram of the same passage, obtained via a method known as the complex wavelet transform. A discussion of wavelet analysis and its many variants is beyond the scope of this Element, but a reasonably layperson-friendly discussion of it can be found in Roads (1996, pp. 581–9). It is the complex wavelet transform (CWT) of the Matlab scientific computing environment that is used here, specifically the Morse wavelet with its default settings.[12] In Figure 24, the structure of the energy distribution over time and frequency of the sample being played, and how it scales as it is played at different pitches, can be much more clearly seen. What is seen confirms what is heard, the same audio being played at different scales (it should be remembered that the term 'scale' here is used in the same sense of the scale of a map, not that of a musical scale comprising different notes, although there is a link between these two meanings, as Figure 24 illustrates). The onsets, the rising pitch and the texture of the sound can all be easily observed.

Following this ratcheting up at the very start, material first heard during the middle eighteen of 'SLAVE' is heard. So far all of the audio has been in mono. After 12 seconds, the signal moves to the left speaker only and then to the right. On the opposite side of this material (so first appearing right then left) is a short, abrupt and acoustically dry rhythmic motif. The sound seems completely alien, yet it is actually a quotation from 'The Fashion Show', specifically the two bars that begin at 0.05,[13] which has been transposed by an extreme amount, twenty-nine semi-tones, which is two octaves plus a perfect fourth. This drastically alters the sound in two ways: it is shortened from being two bars in duration to being less than two crotchets, and the sounds are transposed from being a heterogeneous mix of bass, kick drum, tom and shaker to a much more homogenous sound that is akin to a castanet, in both timbre and the rhythmic figuration that is heard, although some sense of pitch is retained.

This transformation is shown in Figure 25: the top panel is a scalogram of the two bars from the opening of 'The Fashion Show'; the lower panel is a scalogram (with the same parameters) of what is heard as a quasi-castanet

---

[12] https://uk.mathworks.com/help/wavelet/ug/morse-wavelets.html.

[13] The audio that is presented in 'Don't Cry' is without the pad sound that is heard in the two bar section at 0.05 of 'The Fashion Show' in this edition of *Slave*. The extended version of 'The Fashion Show' that is on the alternative edition of the album begins with the exact excerpt (i.e. without the pad) used in 'Don't Cry'.

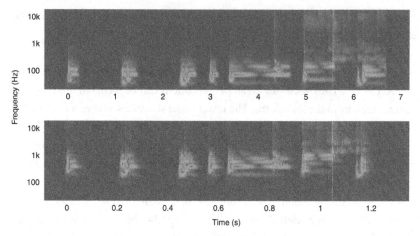

Figure 25 Scalogram of a two-bar excerpt from the opening of 'The Fashion Show' (top) and a two-beat excerpt (bottom) from 'Don't Cry' (timings are relative to start of sample).

timbre in 'Don't Cry'. Although the time and pitch scales are different, the structure of the audio is revealed to be identical: it is a diminution and transposition of material from earlier in the album.

A transcription of three of the parts from this section of 'The Fashion Show' is shown in Figure 26 and the same parts, following diminution and transposition, are shown in Figure 27. Transposition by an octave leads to a doubling in pitch and halving of duration. Therefore, transposition by two octaves results in pitch that is four times higher and a duration that is four times shorter, so two bars of four crotchets becomes two crotchets. However, the total transposition is by two octaves and a perfect fourth. Transposition by a perfect fourth further increases the pitch by a ratio of 4/3 and reduces the duration by a further 3/4, giving one and a half crotchets.

The demisemiquavers in the bass part of Figure 26 are only a few milliseconds in length and so when transposed become perceptually fused with the longer notes that they immediately precede. The three quavers in the second bar of the bass part map to positions that are not on the demisemiquaver grid (although they are depicted as such in the score, for the sake of simplicity): they are on the seventh, but a little behind the eighth and ninth demisemiquavers. Although the patterns are not identical, this recalls the feel of the kick drum pattern from 'SLAVE' shown in Figure 19; the transposition by a perfect fourth, with its 4/3 ratio, effects a rhythmic change that embodies the suppleness of the go-go groove, as well as continuing the emblematic use of this interval in the harmonic organisation of the album. The chromagram (Figure 28) can be

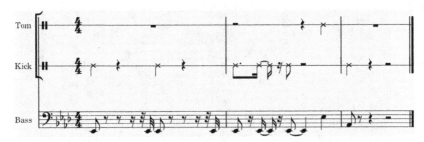

Figure 26 Transcription of kick drum, tom-tom and bass from the opening of 'Fashion Show'.

Figure 27 Diminution and transposition, as heard in 'Don't Cry', of the parts shown in Figure 19.

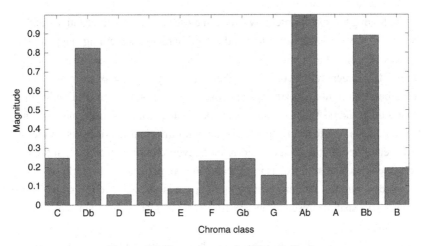

Figure 28 Chromagram for 'Don't Cry'.

interpreted as a hybrid of those for 'The Fashion Show' and 'SLAVE', the Eb and Ab in the former transposed up to Ab and Db and combined with the Eb, Ab and Bb of the latter.

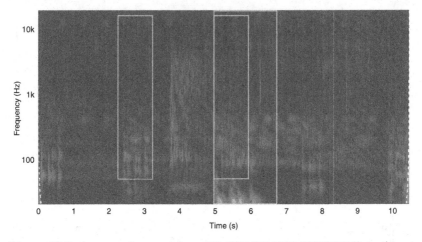

Figure 29 Scalogram of excerpt from 'SLAVE TO THE RHYTHM' starting at
0.36. The two smaller red boxes show material heard at pitch; the larger red box
shows it transposed down by an octave (augmented by a factor of two).

Also within this section, an octave transposition of the audio is heard with
itself, as shown in the scalogram of Figure 29: what was a finger snap is now
more of a slow-motion clap and the triangle part becomes some sort of hybrid of
a gong and a ride cymbal. Rhythmically it creates a disruption of the groove, as
the finger snaps on the second and fourth beats are now heard on the third beat
and only the third beat.

Following the spatial interplay between these two very distinct sounds as they
suddenly swap between the left and right channels, something happens that
makes very clear the spatial advantages of spread, over distinct left/right, stereo:
the ability to generate a complex and enveloping panorama of instruments and
reverberation right across the space between, and sometimes extending beyond,
two loudspeakers. What happens is actually quite simple – the signal switches
from being mono to being spread stereo, with different instruments panned to
different places in the image, decorrelated reverberation sent to each of the two
loudspeakers, and so forth, as is typical of stereo mixes from the early seventies
onwards – but this sudden opening up of space is unusual and dramatic. These
changes in spatial presentation are all effected much faster than those in the
previous track.

Finally, the signal returns to mono before being quickly 'pan scanned'
(moved between loudspeakers) and heavily flanged. Flanging is an effect
created by adding a delayed version of a signal to itself, with the delay being
so short (usually about 10 ms) that it causes timbral rather than temporal
changes to the sound, and varying so that the timbral change is constantly

shifting. Here it is heard as the sweeping sound that gradually descends as the audio fades out.

3.8 Ladies and Gentlemen: Miss Grace Jones

This is the piece that was released as the single 'Slave to the Rhythm', although here it also features a short spoken introduction by McShane, who briefly returns to introduce Jones. He is heard in mono, without reverberation, and at a noticeably higher level than his monologue that opens the album. Much of what has been heard already is combined here in the final assemblage of the material that Horn and his performance and production team played, captured and constructed in the nine months of its production. For example, the 'show me' pad, constructed on Andy Richard's Fairlight CMI, that first appeared briefly in 'The Fashion Show' now outlines the chorus harmonies in this piece's introduction, which are those that first emerged at the end of 'Frog and Princess'.

The orchestra appears for the first time since the opening piece of the album. The arrangement is by Richard Niles, who has described the extravagance with which he was encouraged by Horn to approach the scoring:

> What I originally said to Trevor is 'what do you want on it?' and he said the words 'impress me'. That is a red rag to a bull to say that to Richard Niles. So, what I had was full jazz big band plus a full string section and then, of course, we had brass and woodwinds as well and some percussion, marimbas, stuff like that, so it was pretty big. (Niles in Allinson and Levine, 2006)

Table 1 outlines the structure of the song. There is an uncontrived malleability to this structure, for example in the three-beat bar in the second verse and an ambiguity as to whether sections plus bridges are 16 + 4 or 18 + 2 bars, which is evocative of the improvised nature of go-go. A choir (The Ambrosian Singers) enters in bar 8, but is this at the end of the introduction or the beginning of the bridge? There is also, as shown in Figure 30, a less rigid pulse. This is no doubt due to the use of longer rhythmic phrases from the original go-go recordings, which have variations of tempo within them (and possibly between players in the ensemble at particular instants, too). There is no longer the machine-like adherence to an utterly constant tempo that is heard, for example, in 'The Fashion Show', and this can be seen in the tempo profile in Figure 30.

The chromagram for this piece is shown in Figure 31. In this analysis of *Slave*, chromagrams have been presented for each of the eight pieces, and it is instructive to observe how they change between them. They have been used here because the key centres in *Slave* are generally consistent (either Eb or Ab) but somewhat vague in their role or strength in each of the pieces. This is because of the use of frequent non-diatonic harmonies and sus-4 chords in place

Table 1 Structure of 'Ladies and Gentlemen' (four crotchets to a bar unless indicated)

Bars	Section	Lyric	Notes
1–4	Introduction (chorus)	'Ladies and gentlemen . . .' (spoken)	Mono, no reverberation
5–8		'Slave to the rhythm'	'Show me' sampled pad
9–12	Bridge to verse	'Oh, baby . . .'	Choir enters briefly, bar 8
13–20	Verse 1	'Work all day . . .'	Antiphonal rhythm guitar parts begin in left and right channels
21–28	Bridge to chorus	'Never stop . . .'	Strings enter
29–39	Chorus	'Work to the rhythm . . .'	11 bar structure (4 + 4 + 1 + 2)
40–51	Verse 2	'Axe to wood . . .'	With orchestra and choir
			Bar 45 is three crotchets long
52–59	Bridge to chorus	'Never stop . . .'	Rhythmic decaying delays on backing vocal 'keep it up'
60–71	Chorus	'Breathe to the rhythm . . .'	Pan flute melody enters (possibly 'Caliope' [sic] DX–7 preset)
72–75	Bridge to middle 8	'Oh, baby . . .'	
76–83	Middle 8	'Don't cry . . .'	Begins with chord IV (Db) followed by Neapolitan sixth, flattened II (Bbb, enharmonically A)
84–91	Chorus	'We live . . .'	
92–94	Bridge to finale	'And now . . .'	Three bars in length
95–102	Finale	'Slave, to the rhythm . . .'	Decaying crotchet delay on 'ooh'

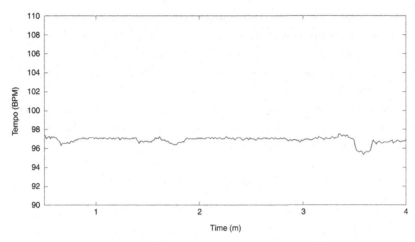

Figure 30 Tempo profile of main body of 'Ladies and Gentlemen'.

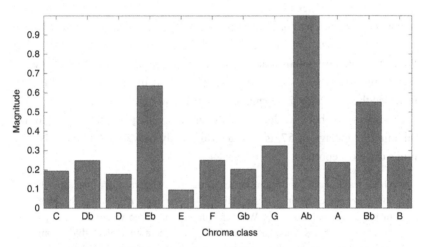

Figure 31 Chromagram for 'Ladies and Gentlemen'.

of triads on these notes. For example, it is not always clear whether one (Ab) is the subdominant to the other's tonic (Eb), or whether the relationship is dominant (Eb) to tonic (Ab). Chromagrams offer a straightforward insight into two things: which pitches are particularly strongly weighted and the shape of the distribution in general. A sparse chromagram indicates a relatively simple harmonic scheme; a more evenly distributed pattern suggests more complex harmony (or a significant non-pitched element, such as loud percussion) (Jensen and Herbert, 2016, pp. 287–8). Whilst these diagrams provide useful general information about the distribution of energy in each piece across pitch chroma, it is important not to draw simplistic conclusions, such as assuming that the most energetic chroma is definitely the key of the piece (although it would certainly make it a reasonable candidate). It is best to use these to observe how the spectrum of pitches changes between pieces on the album, even though the tonal centres seem quite consistent throughout.

And so, after almost 38 minutes, we arrive at the end of a production that took nine months to complete. In the next section, we will look at the intersections of culture within which that production took place.

4 Crossing Two: Culture

4.1 Celebrity Culture

As well as the release of *Slave to the Rhythm*, 1985 also saw Grace Jones star in a James Bond film: *A View to a Kill* (Broccoli and Wilson, 1985). Her character, May Day, is a brutal henchwoman who sees the light at the end of the film when she realises she has been betrayed by her lover, who is the central villain. That villain was originally to have been played by David Bowie and then, when he was not available, by Sting (Bowie in Shaar-Murray, 1984). Christopher Walken eventually took the part, but the casting aspirations serve as an illustration of the relationship between popular film and music (Duran Duran also provided the music for the opening credits) at that time.

The interaction between Jones and Roger Moore, playing James Bond for the final time at the age of 57, is reported differently by various individuals. The film's director reports:

> Grace was a playful and enthusiastic character ... She was more than a match for Roger and came up with a practical joke even more devastating than one of his traditional stunts ... We were filming the scene where Roger slips between the sheets when Grace suddenly produced a huge black dildo from under the covers. She was screaming with laughter for about 10 minutes, although I'm not sure Roger saw the funny side. (Glen, 2001, p. 160)

Jones recalls: 'I got on great with Roger Moore. He was very funny and easy going. He helped me a lot, because I wanted so much to be good. I was a worrier. I worried that I didn't know what I was doing. When I got stuck he would humour me' (Jones, 2015, p. 277).

This is rather in contrast to Moore's take on working with her:

> I'm afraid my diplomatic charm was stretched to the limit with Grace. Every day in her dressing room – which was adjacent to mine – she played very loud music. I was not a fan of heavy metal ... One day I snapped. I marched into her room, pulled the plug out and then went back to my room, picked up a chair and flung it at the wall. The dent is still there.

There is also his response to the dildo prank, 'I'm glad she thought it was funny', which concisely summarises this clash of personalities and cultures (Moore, 2008, p. 257).

The interaction between Jones and Moore, and the worlds that they represent, is one of the many crossings that exist with *Slave* and its protagonist (credited as 'breath, blood and voice' on the album's sleeve) that have a cultural basis. The term culture is used here in its broadest sense: 'the way of life, especially the general customs and beliefs, of a particular group of people at a particular time' (Cambridge Dictionary, n.d.). Moore, the suave but now ageing and somewhat old-fashioned, privileged, white, male product of RADA, playing heroes of the early and mid-twentieth century, such as Simon Templar (*The Saint*) and James Bond in mainstream film and TV action drama, meets Jones, the loud, adventurous, black, female, queer icon. 'Sparks will fly', as the *Slave* lyric goes. Moore was not the only establishment figure she had brushed up against. She had notoriously challenged British chat show host Russell Harty for patronising and ignoring her on a primetime BBC broadcast in 1980. And yet she was in a James Bond film and on the Russell Harty show because she had crossed over and broadened her appeal outside of the gay clubs in which she had first performed as a singer. This star status is directly acknowledged in the first edition of *Slave* when a sycophantic interviewer is heard commenting on her appearance in *A View to a Kill*, at the very of end of 'Jones The Rhythm'.

A more orthodox and good-humoured interview took place on *The Tonight Show Starring Johnny Carson* in May 1985 in the United States. In the interview Carson raises the topic of the contretemps with Harty and discusses the James Bond film (which was released in the States two weeks afterwards). He also holds up a copy of the front of the vinyl LP sleeve for *Slave*, a whole five months before recording for the album was completed. When she is introduced, she enters to an energetic big band performance, confident and enjoying the attention, and this was something that directly inspired Horn:

> I saw Grace on a talk show in America and I thought 'that's obviously the way to do it, we'll have a talk show thing at the end, 'here's Grace, slave to the rhythm!', that will give us our climax. And I said to her 'I want you to act as if you're on the Johnny Carson Show and he's just announced you' . . . And she just went out and did it. (Horn in Allinson and Levine, 2006)

Jones has remarked that *Slave* 'turned out to be like an autobiography of my voice, and what I had been through to become the singer I wanted to be' (Jones, 2015, p. 284). The 'here's Grace' becomes the arrival point of that journey, the triumphant entrance on the Carson show to promote a much-anticipated film that she was starring in, with Carson showing the audience the sleeve of the record that had not yet been completed and would include an homage to that very moment, of the crossing into global fame.

Jones had arrived in the United States from Jamaica at the age of thirteen, following her parents who had relocated there a few years earlier. Her father was a minister and established an Apostolic Church in Syracuse, New York. She was relieved to escape her life in Jamaica, where overbearing and abusive guardians made her feel that she had been 'crushed under the bible' (Jones, 2015, p. 4). Her brother Chris, a gifted pianist, was prevented from being involved in church music-making when rumours that he was gay circulated in the congregation and reached his father. Jones explains that his gender and sexuality, as well as hers, were more nuanced and fluid than the binary distinctions of heterosexual and homosexual. 'Chris was never the same when [the church music] was taken away from him. He would say "Well, if I'm gay I'll do what gay people do". And I'd go with him to the clubs. Being tangled up, having some of the man in me, I loved that. The man in me – as well as the girl – loved men!' (p. 48).

She began modelling and acting in Philadelphia and New York before moving to Paris. She had auditioned for 'Philly Soul' producers Gamble and Huff, singing a song from a play she was performing in, but it had gone badly. In Paris she had taken to impromptu performances of song and dance (she had worked as a go-go dancer in Philadelphia[14]) when socialising. She recorded a demo, was encouraged to take singing lessons, but she was uncomfortable with her singing teacher and with her voice. However, early recordings that she had made in Paris found their way to Tom Moulton in New York. Moulton had started his music career constructing continuous mixes of music for dance clubs, using assemble editing techniques with a record player and a Revox analogue tape machine (Burns, 2013). This technique was innovative at the time, and he began to receive offers of editing and production work within the emerging disco scene whose aesthetic his work was doing so much to shape (Burns, 2013).

Although her voice was still limited ('I hear my early records now and think, *Jesus Christ, I am so off-key!*' (Jones, 2015, p. 216)), the Moulton disco sound of her records and the theatrical cabaret of her live performances led to success and notoriety. Moulton describes a performance that she gave in a gay members-only disco in New York in 1977: 'All of a sudden the spotlight hits her. She starts singing "I Need a Man", and the place goes crazy. After she finishes, she goes, "I don't know about you, honey, but I need a fucking man!" Talk about a room-worker. Whatever it takes. She was so determined' (Moulton in Walters, 2015b).

---

[14] Go-go dancer is a general term applied to someone paid to dance in nightclubs. It is not related at all to the go-go musical genre that emerged in the late seventies and early eighties.

In 1980, after three albums with Moulton, Jones began work with producers Chris Blackwell (also the founder of Island Records, with whom she was signed) and Alex Sadkin. The band that she worked with included the drum and bass partnership of Sly Dunbar and Robbie Shakespeare, and the sound that Blackwell aimed for was more inclusive of Jones' personality and arguably better suited to her voice.

> We recorded from scratch, as live as possible. It was very exciting because I had had the wisdom to get Alex Sadkin as the engineer at Compass Point Studios (in Nassau, The Bahamas, where these albums were recorded). He was beyond compare for his talent, his taste, his ear. The record needed someone fantastically fluid at mixing on the go, to capture the groove as it was happening, mostly played live, to give the process a certain balance and coherence ... You'd never been exposed to that kind of thing before, but it suited your personality and that in turn influenced the direction of your music. (Blackwell in Jones, 2015, p. 221)

Three albums were recorded with this team of producers and performers: *Warm Leatherette* (Jones, 1980), *Nightclubbing* (Jones, 1981) and *Living My Life* (Jones, 1982). Whilst the songs (many of them cover versions) originate from a variety of genres, as they are rendered on these albums they have a sparse, rhythm-orientated sonic identity. Just before recording *Warm Leatherette* she gave birth to a son, Paulo. His father was Jean-Paul Goude, the artist and designer, with whom Jones had a personal relationship from the late seventies to the early eighties, and a professional relationship that endured beyond that. Goude created the cover art for each of the Compass Point recordings (including *Blue Black in Black on Brown* for *Nightclubbing*, mentioned in the previous section), and *Slave*, as well as directing some of her stage shows and videos. Excerpts of Goude's recollections of that relationship from his book, *Jungle Fever*, are heard in the piece 'The Frog and The Princess' and appear on the album sleeve.

Goude's work and his book are certainly controversial. They have been described as exploitative and distasteful, and the distinction between art and pornography is not always clear. The cover of the book features a picture of Jones naked in a cage. One retrospective view of this is that 'we've come at least some way as a society since Jean-Paul Goude's day. But how long will it be before we automatically recognize any picture of a black woman caged up like an animal as offensive?' (Sauers, 2009). Goude has acknowledged the controversy with regard to race: 'I find myself in a strange situation, because on the one hand the liberal is embarrassed by my attitude, while racists ironically interpret me as one of them' (Goude, 1981, p. 107). His work *White and Black* (Goude, 1983) is a striking representation of their collaboration, for better and/or for worse.

As Warner notes, Goude's manipulated photographic image for the cover of *Slave* can be seen as a visual analogy of sampling (Warner, 2003, p. 131). However, here the manipulations are in the analogue domain; the first version of Photoshop, for the editing and manipulation of digital images, did not appear until two years after the release of the record. As Goude states, 'I saw her as the ideal vehicle for my work', and it seems that Horn did so too, able, like Goude, to work with the grain of her talents: 'Grace is pretty off the wall anyway and how she presented herself suggested to me that she should be handled rather like an art object' (Horn in Cunningham, 1998, p. 308). This approach was appreciated by Jones:

> I had never worked with anyone like Trevor. He allowed me to experiment with my voice in a way no one had before. He let me be free to try things out in every part of the song. To attack, to be sweet, to be operatic, and then he pieced all of these fragments together . . . He totally got it . . . Trevor did to my voice what Jean-Paul did to my face and body. (Jones, 2015, pp. 282–4)

Lipson has estimated that Jones herself spent as many hours working on the album as he and Horn had spent months on the project – nine – (Lindvall, 2012), and yet it is hard to imagine that the album would have been plausible without her voice, her image and her history being so present within it. There is also the issue of the budget, which Jones says she was ultimately responsible for paying and was 'gigantic'. The exact budget for the album is unknown (a figure of £385,00 is often reported, but all of those reports appear to derive from a Wikipedia article that does not provide a citation for that figure). What is known is that work on the entire album lasted for nine months. It was an odyssey that Bruce Woolley has said was begun when Chris Blackwell heard Goude's comment on the first ('Jones the Rhythm') version that 'you could sell a black groove to a white man, but you couldn't sell a white groove to a black man' (Walters, 2015a). Lipson explains that a series of experiments then followed before the final go-go version was arrived at: 'really, the whole album is a collection of experiments in which we were trying to create a good single' (Tingen, 1987, p. 55). Jones claims that Horn had heard Chuck Brown and The Soul Searcher's 'We Need Some Money' and based his arrangement of 'Ladies and Gentlemen' on its drum pattern. Horn has described how the vocals for the go-go version of the song ('Ladies and Gentlemen' on the album) came together.

> She was three days late . . . but, boy, talk about a good actress! When we played her the song . . . she was saying 'this is not the same song. this is a different song, I thought we'd recorded this song' so I said 'it's changed a bit' . . . she sat down and she said 'it's been a long day in the fields and I'm really tired, I've been working all day and I'm sitting on the veranda and the sun's going down',

and I was going [to the session engineers] 'get the microphone. Get the microphone!' ... Bruce whispered the lines into her ear: 'work all day' .... 'as men who know'. She just sort of sung the song ... I do remember that Steve and I were jubilant, we were jumping up and down in the control room like: 'yes! It's gonna work!' (Horn in Allinson and Levine, 2006)

4.2 Musical Culture

As discussed in Section 2, the arrival of digital sampling technologies in the early 1980s transformed the audio fabric of the production process and the ways in which that process could access and shape it. 'Sampling stands alongside allusion, quotation, and reinterpretation as part of the modern musician's toolkit ... As a technique sampling reflects the ingenious innovations of musicians across geography (especially the Black Atlantic) and genres' (McLeod and Dicola, 2011, p. 73). Speaking mainly from the perspective of the hip-hop canon, McLeod and Dicola identify the half-decade between 1987 and 1992 as a golden age of sampling, when the technology and the culture for groundbreaking music existed, but copyright law had yet to catch up and put a brake on it.

Slave was produced two years before the dawn of this era. It used equipment that, because of sheer cost, was out of reach of most studios and producers and certainly not available to nascent underground scenes, at least not with sufficient access and expertise. For example, the studio that Afrika Bambaataa and The Soul Sonic Force used for 'Planet Rock' (1982) did have an early CMI but, according to producer Arthur Baker, there was no expertise available to capture new samples with it: 'all we used was the explosion and the orchestra hit [factory samples that shipped with the instrument]. The Fairlight was a $100,000 waste of space' (Baker in Brewster and Broughton, 2018). 'Planet Rock' led to proceedings from lawyers representing Kraftwerk's publishing company. Kraftwerk were the originators of both 'Trans Europe Express', from which the new record took its main melody, and 'Numbers', from which its programmed groove was emulated on a Roland TR-808 drum machine. Perhaps ironically, given the presence of early sampling technology in the studio where the record was made, it was publishing (i.e. the rights to the melody and the rhythm arrangement) rather than mechanical copyright on which the proceedings were based. Nevertheless, this idea of borrowing and combining to create novelty, which sampling technology would turn out to be so suited to exploring, was emerging from the DJ culture of the time:

I used to hear 'Trans-Europe Express' all over the place. In playgrounds, clubs, everywhere ... Then 'Numbers' came out. I used to hang out at a record store in Brooklyn called Music Factory, and the guys who later became Rockers Revenge ... worked there, and they turned me on to things. I came in and heard 'Numbers' and they said, 'Oh man, it's flying out of the store.' So, me and Bam decided to mix the two together. (Baker in Brewster and Broughton, 2018)

Slave does not directly quote existing musical ideas or actual audio from the compositions and recordings of others (aside from a fleeting trumpet riff heard at 2.13 in 'Jones the Rhythm' that closely resembles the main theme of the final movement of Bach's second Brandenburg Concerto), but it does do so extensively from itself. Of course, it borrows an entire class of timbral-rhythmic patterning – the go-go groove – and to achieve this it does directly sample go-go musicians. However, these are session players on the record itself who are briefed, recorded and paid before their work is sifted and fashioned using the techniques and technologies described in previous sections. It is the budget and the process of the production, described in the previous section, that makes such a rich body of audio material available and amenable to manipulation by technology, without the need to go outside of the production itself for the source material with which to work.

Slave itself has been sampled many times. In the years since the first edition's release in 1985, the economics of music technology have changed dramatically. Cheaper samplers, such as the Emulator and Ensoniq Mirage, were already available in 1985, albeit without the flexibility of the Fairlight and Synclavier systems of the time. Paul Hardcastle had used an Emulator for a sampled stutter that was the hook for his 1985 single '19' (Hardcastle, 1985). In 1986 Akai released the S900, a rack-mount (i.e. keyboard-less but controllable via MIDI) sampler offering sonic quality similar to the earlier Fairlight CMI, although not the CD quality of the series III. The S900 had a retail price of £1500 (about £5000 in today's prices), which signalled how sampling was becoming increasingly affordable, costing as much as a second-hand car, rather than a house). The increasing integration in the nineties of tools for digital music production into software that could be run on home computers (the harnessing of cheap general-purpose computing hardware and operating systems discussed in Section 2) meant that highly sophisticated sampling technology was available to most for negligible cost.

In 1989 The Orb, a group strongly associated with the chill out genre that emerged alongside acid house, released 'A Huge Ever Growing Pulsating Brain That Rules From The Centre Of The Ultraworld' (The Orb, 1989). The single featured a largely unaltered sample of the choir from *Slave*, which is heard briefly in 'Ladies and Gentlemen' but more extensively and (crucially for sampling) in isolation at the beginning of 'SLAVE'. The piece also featured a sample of Minnie Riperton's 'Loving You'. At the time the Orb comprised

Alex Patterson (its longstanding member) and Jimmy Caulty (who left soon after the release of this single). Caulty was a member of the KLF, who 'were among the first to widely circulate self-conscious critiques of copyright, authorship and ownership to a broad audience' (McLeod and Dicola, 2011, p. 72). Legal action led to the Ripperton sample being replaced with a soundalike, but the lengthy quotation from *Slave* remains. Alongside another single by the group, 'Little Fluffy Clouds' (The Orb, 1990), which sampled Steve Reich's *Electric Counterpoint* (Metheny, 1989) and a radio interview with Rickie Lee Jones, and The KLF's *Chillout* album, which sampled Elvis Presley amongst many others (The KLF, 1990), 'Ultraworld' has become a part of the electronic dance (and dance-related) repertory. Intertextuality works in both directions: quoting from a work imbues the work in which it is quoted with some of its character and so affects its reception by the listener, but the reception of the quoted work is also changed. *Slave* is now partly 'that record that was sampled by The Orb'.

Perhaps because of the way it explores itself in making repeated use of material in different contexts and sometimes in isolation, *Slave* has been sampled extensively. In particular, Ian McShane's opening monologue has found its way into the productions of others. David Harness' 'The Rhythm', released on a Moulton Records[15] compilation *Miami South Beach Sessions 2016*, is a typical example, an instrumental deep house record that features short, repeated excerpts (Harness, 2008). Liaisons D's 'The Rhythm' also places excerpts over an otherwise instrumental dance piece (Liaisons D, 1992). Mastergroove's 'Anialate' features the pitched down 'annihilating the rhythm' of 'Operattack', as does Red Princess' 'You Make Me Feel So Good' (Mastergroove, 2012; Red Princess, 1993). The list goes on and on. The idea of sampling Johnny Carson saying 'here's Johnny!' at the opening 'The Motorcade Sped On' released by Steinski in 1986 (of Steinski and Double D fame via *The Lessons*) follows the evocation of Carson's show in the 'Here's Grace!' of 'Ladies and Gentlemen' (Steinski and The Mass Media, 1986).

Like the opening of 'Apache' (Michael Viner's Incredible Bongo Band, 1973) or the drum break from 'Amen, Brother' (The Winstons, 1969), these samples seem to have an immediate accessibility due to the isolation from other components of the track from which they are being sampled, along with a particular, desirable quality (of groove, in the case of 'Amen, Brother' and 'Apache', of relevance and quality of capture in the case of 'Jones the Rhythm').

It is, partly, the way in which the material in *Slave* is arranged and presented, at the beginning of the era of straightforward and flexible direct quotation, that

---

[15] Not connected with Tom Moulton, but possibly named in tribute to him.

has led to its embedding in so much of the sample-based music that has followed it, its relevance broadened and elevated by its subsequent quotations. It is over thirty-five years old. The same temporal distance exists between now and the album's first release as exists between it and Perry Como's 1949 recording of 'Some Enchanted Evening'. *Slave* is no longer a contemporary pop record, even if in some ways it sounds like one. Yet it reverberates still; Jones was still performing the single as recently as three years ago, and samples from it have been incorporated into an extraordinary number of records by other artists.

5 Crossing Three: Form

5.1 Popular and Art Music

Much has been written about the relative merits of pop and ('classical') art music, and much of that debate is focussed on form (e.g. Adorno, 1941, and Middleton, 1983). In some musicology of pop music there is more of a focus on context (e.g. the society, and its values, within which the music was created) rather than the text (the actual sounds, pitches etc. within the music itself). Richard Middleton is wary of this trend: 'the danger here is that the specifically musical processes – the ways in which sound are combined in this particular song – are ignored. This then tends to confirm the view of popular music's aesthetic poverty' (Middleton, 1999, p. 142). The cultural and musical theorist Theodor Adorno had much to say on this matter, and Middleton's distillation of Adorno's position is that 'popular music is deficient because its forms are predictable and schematic, whereas in "serious" music, by contrast the form of a piece is individual – worked out afresh in each case so that all the details interrelate and cohere' (142).

In the comparison of popular and art song that opens his analysis of Joni Mitchell's music, Whitesell gives the following descriptions that are typically associated with high art: 'serious, edifying; profound; complex, subtle; carefully constructed; enduring in value, establishing a cultural heritage'. For 'low or popular art' he gives 'entertaining; vital, authentic; simple, common; spontaneous, immediate; novel, topical in value' (Whitesell, 2008, p. 8). He notes that classical music does not always avoid the simple, and that the creators of popular music often exhibit refinement and 'attention to craft'. However, the term craft is itself loaded: 'craft is the power to produce a preconceived result by consciously controlled action: the craftsman always knows what he wants to make in advance' (Rogers, 1983, p. 58), implying an artisanal rather than artistic process, and this returns us to form, the structural templates within which music is constructed and the extent to which they are original and adaptive to the materials they contain. What Middleton is warning against is an undue focus on the social contexts, rather than the sounds, of popular music, as a way of sidestepping the issue of form.

This Element is concerned with both the nature of the music of *Slave* itself and the context in which it was created. It is interested in both why it came to be created and how that creation is constructed in the tangible artefact, the audio recording. To that end, it has focussed on a detailed analysis of the text (i.e. the audio), combining both listening and computer-aided analysis and using score- and audio-level depictions, in the third section. However. the technological, economic and cultural contexts – the identities and capabilities of the human and non-human agents involved in its creation – have also been considered in the two sections that appear before and after that central analysis. The analysis reveals two contrasting influences on the production: the amount of time and technological resources available for experimentation, to get it right, along with limitations such as memory for storing samples of that technology. These give rise to a particular deployment and redeployment of material within its form. The result is an intriguing mix of popular and art form, something that seems best described as cyclic recycling.

5.2 The Intensional and the Extensional

Chester (1970, pp. 78–9) suggests: 'Western classical music is the apodigm of the extensional form of musical construction ... Rock however follows, like many non-European musics, the path of intensional development', which is of direct relevance to the discussion of form in this section. *Slave* is an instructive work with which to explore Chester's fundamental statement, that art music expresses itself via changes in, and developments of, simple atoms that occur over the duration of a movement or piece, whereas in rock (and, by generalising outside of his particular focus, popular) music the carrier of meaning or function is within the 'modulation of the basic notes and by inflexion of the basic beat' (p. 79). Tagg provides the polar examples of sonata form – 'more likely to derive interest from the presentation of ideas over a duration of several minutes' (Tagg, 2013, p. 272), and the short, repeated riff that is heard from the very opening of '(I Can't Get No) Satisfaction' (The Rolling Stones, 1965). He also highlights its relationship to the extended present, which has 'an objective existence inside the human brain' in the form of its working memory (Tagg, 2013, p. 273). For a discussion of groove in relation to this experience of the present, recall the quote from Anne Danielson in Section 3 and the 'presence in the here and now of the event' (Danielson, 2010) of the listener.

Allan Moore also emphasises the extensional and intensional of Chester as poles of a continuum and provides examples of intensional (the performer of

Mozart, making micro changes to the timing and tuning of what is explicitly specified in the score, in order to express their response to it) and extensional (the use of substitute harmonies in Howlin' Wolf's 'Little Red Rooster') development within pieces that primarily exhibit the opposite tendencies (Moore, 2001, pp. 22–4). As Wishart and Virden (1977, p. 162) point out, Chester uses the term 'modulation' loosely. His likely meaning is of tuning (including dynamically, i.e. bending) of individual notes, rather than the more specific and established musical meaning, of shifting to a different tonal centre over time rather than instantaneously, which is something that is more common in extensional development.

Chester is also not specific about what inflections he refers to: those that happen within the same epoch of extended time and are then repeated in the same form throughout, or those that occur differently through the course of a piece, or both. It seems most likely that he is referring to the former, the repeating nature of a consistently played groove, intra-epoch inflections that are maintained between them. But since the genre he explicitly deals with is rock, inter-epoch variations in the groove may also be covered by his definition. This, of course, would be an extensional development of an intensional feature. Chester's classifications are illuminating, but they are best considered as polarised ideals of different types of presentation and development of musical material that typically occur within art or popular musics, but usually with some elements of each in both.

5.3 Form in *Slave to the Rhythm*

As I have alluded to in previous sections, the recording technology used in *Slave* enabled the mutability of its structure and contents to persist until the very end of the production and post-production process. As the composer, sound artist and audio designer Trevor Wishart had noted not ten years before,

> In the modern recording studio, with its multi-tracking facilities, we can lay down one track at a time, performing each line over and over again until it is judged, aurally, to be precisely what we desire, until the direct musical experience resulting from the musical action is thoroughly and precisely refined through direct unmediated reference to that, now repeatable, experience. Similarly, the tape composer can work directly with the whole gamut of sound materials ... We can compose directly in experiential time. (Wishart, 1977, p. 148)

The digital studio that was emerging at the time of the album's creation offered still finer control over sonic materials.

It is certain that the final form of *Slave* is not what was originally intended. The commission to Horn was to produce one single for Island Records, her final release of new material for that label before moving to EMI/Manhattan (Jones, 2015, p. 300). But Horn's dissatisfaction with the original version had led him to pursue the go-go version of the song. It is not clear when his mind changed about the original version, perhaps after the orchestral parts had been scored and recorded, but he has said:

> I still like the Germanic first version. Because we had two highly contrasting versions, we thought it might be worth going further with some other approaches to the same song. This was recorded at the commercial peak for twelve-inch mixes, so instead of having an album of different songs, we could present an album which was really an overblown twelve-inch. (Horn in Cunningham, 1998, pp. 308–9)

Jones has a slightly different view: 'It wasn't a single, it wasn't an album. Trevor had delivered this selection of tracks that derived from the original song, not a collection of remixes, but the same song variously extended and rewritten so that it became a number of songs' (Jones, 2015, p. 301).

Although not by design, the unique circumstances (a final single for Jones that Horn wanted to be timeless and to get just right) and technological process – 'I did nearly the whole album on the Synclavier' (Lipson in Tingen, 1987, p. 55) – contrived to create a form that manages to hit close to the centre of Chester's extensional/intensional continuum.

Within each of the pieces, different grooves are established that are largely intensional (there is some variation in the patterning in 'SLAVE', for example, as discussed in Section 3) but are extensional variations of the go-go groove (which appears on four of the eight pieces) when considered across the whole album. The first appearance, in 'The Fashion Show', has an utterly consistent metronomic pulse, a relatively sparse kick drum part and a foregrounded cowbell. The second appearance, in 'SLAVE TO THE RHYTM', changes the emphasis on the first beat of the bar. In the third appearance, the way it occupies space is dramatically altered and it is heard in diminution, augmentation and transposition against itself. Finally, the go-go recordings from New York are heard, edited and shaped, but with less rigid technological intervention than previously and therefore with a more elastic tempo.

The organisation of the lyrics crudely follows a sonata form. The majority of the lyric is heard in 'Jones the Rhythm' and is recapitulated in 'Ladies and Gentlemen: Miss Grace Jones', augmented with the new material that has appeared in the intervening pieces (such as the phrase 'don't cry, it's only the rhythm' in 'The Fashion Show', and 'you work all day, as men who know' in 'SLAVE'). 'Operattack' uses utterances taken solely from 'Jones the Rhythm' (except for 'annihilating rhythm', spoken by McShane, which appears as part of the quotation from Penman on the album's sleeve but not in his monologue at beginning of 'Jones the Rhythm'). It is the one piece on the album whose intra-piece form is more extensional than intensional. The material from *Jungle Fever* is only heard in 'The Frog and The Princess', whereas all of the other lyrical content is shared between two or more pieces.

Common harmonic elements are shared between many pieces, but they are not just repetitions of the same scheme. For example, the harmony of the chorus of 'Ladies and Gentlemen', first heard in the opening on the 'show me' pad, is what eventually emerges from the development that occurs over the last minute and a half of 'Frog and Princess'. The interval of the perfect fourth crops up throughout, from the figure heard at the very start of 'Jones the Rhythm', through the regular appearance of the IV to I (Ab to Eb) progression, often with sus-4 versions of those chords (often with the fourth emphasised, for example the rhythm guitar playing Ab over Eb in the left channel in the verse of 'Ladies and Gentlemen'), to the pentatonic parallel fourths in 'The Crossing', to the two-octaves-plus-a-fourth transposition of the 'The Fashion Show' within 'Don't Cry'. The record ends in Ab and begins in Eb.

The treatment of space is both intensional and extensional. Spatial position and movement are also a part of groove (an obvious example of this is the literal placement within a stereo image of the different components of the drum kit, which enables us to sense the relationship of the rhythmic expression with the different limbs of the body). Through arrangement and mixing (of which spatial positioning is a crucial element), the audibility of different components of timbres and grooves is controlled, and hierarchies of sounds are created. The use of space within pieces then becomes part of its intensional development. The changing relationships in space that occur from piece to piece as seen, for example, in the phase scopes of Section 3, and Warner's observations of how the 'left/right' spatial axis is explored, are more extensional; the changes in the use of space in each piece are one of the developments of the go-go groove throughout.

The form of *Slave* is cyclic, since each piece shares material with others and that material is changed in meaningful ways, albeit not in ways that are typical of the extensional works of art music. The tape machine and the sampler permit this development and working out of the material to take place on the audio itself. The digital data from which the sound of the music are directly derived are refashioned and recycled not just within one piece but across the whole record. The fact that the final form and format of *Slave* is not as originally intended should not detract from the impressive success of that form. It does not matter that it was arrived at iteratively and due to unusual creative and economic factors.

This element has focussed on the abridged edition in part because it is the most limited in the raw materials that it uses. The purpose of this edition, and whether it is the one preferred by its creators, is uncertain, although it was the last edition of it that they produced. Given the time expended on the record up to that point, it seems reasonable to wonder that it might have been, given everything at their disposal and how far they had come, what they had 'judged, *aurally*, to be precisely what we desire'.

6 Intersections and Transitions

The preceding pages have presented an analysis of Grace Jones' *Slave to the Rhythm*, specifically the second edition (Jones, 1987), along with some of the technological and cultural contexts within which it was created and currently exists. Artistic greatness is an intangible, elusive thing to define. In fact, without accepting axioms specific to one culture or another, at the expense of others, it is impossible to identify and it is futile to attempt to do so. The canon of western acoustic art music, which presents us with 'the great composers' and 'classic' works, is something that emerged in the eighteenth century, with repertory as one its precursors (Weber, 1999). For recorded and produced music, the maintenance of, and easy access to, a vast repertory has become straightforward and ubiquitous (consider the vast catalogues that exist within music streaming services such as Spotify, Boomplay and Tidal). It remains to be seen how this will affect the music, if any, from this era and area that is selected, studied and revered in two centuries' time. This Element makes no claim regarding this work's 'greatness' or canonical status. However, thirty-five years on from (the second edition's) release, the single from the album (Jones, 1985a) remains in the repertory. For example, it has been streamed more than five million times via Spotify,[16] a streaming service that began twenty-five years after that record's release.

So why is this particular audio production of broader relevance or interest to our understanding of pop music? Why bother to study to study it at the level of detail afforded in the previous pages? The work of Trevor Horn and Stephen Lipson, particularly from this era, is of interest because of the conjunction of money (enabling both time and technology to be lavished on productions to a greater degree than normal), a willingness to experiment (with form, as well as with technology) and considerable commercial success (particularly with Frankie Goes to Hollywood). For Horn, it seems to represent the apotheosis of these explorations in pop production technique he began more than five years before:

> T.W.: Slave to the Rhythm seems to be a kind of culmination of your work up
> to that point – do you see it like this?
> T.H.: Yes, it was the end of an era, I calmed down after that. I had to get a bit
> more sensible … The fact that Slave to the Rhythm didn't get to number one

---

[16] https://open.spotify.com/artist/2f9ZiYA2ic1r1voObUimdd.

everywhere was the beginning of a certain kind of decline. Which is a bit of
a relief you know. (Horn in Warner, 2003, p. 156)

Horn has continued to produce and did return to this style of production briefly
in 1999 for The Art of Noise's *The Seduction of Claude Debussy* (The Art of
Noise, 1999) but otherwise has produced acts that would be considered more
mainstream (e.g. Cher, Rod Stewart, Robbie Williams, Boyzone) with a more
conservative production style. Yet, for many he remains 'the one producer who
defined the lavish sound Eighties pop more than any other' (Cunningham, 1998,
p. 299). This Element is the most detailed published analysis yet undertaken of
this record that Horn claims as the culmination of his more experimental work
of the eighties.

As described in Section 2, the transition from analogue to digital technology
occurred over a number of years, and it happened in a multitude of different
ways. The emerging technology had its affordances (e.g. the ability to instantly
trigger and transpose any captured sound) but also its limitations (e.g. the length
of sampled sound that could be stored, and its fidelity). The detailed analysis of
the text, at both a signal and higher (e.g. pitch, rhythm) level, provides new
examples of how the crossing from analogue to digital technology changed the
processes and outcomes of the production process. In particular, it demonstrates
how the sampler was able to contribute new forms of quotation and transformation of material. It also shows how material could be forced into more rigid
structures as a result of those processes. The go-go groove existing at various
points between temporally flexible and metronomic throughout the album is an
example of this. The shifts in the timbres of staple pop instruments, such as the
electric piano, are also observed.

This analysis has also sought to show how a greater range of signal processing tools can be used to give new, objective insight into the nature of musical
audio signals. In particular, specific tools have been developed and applied to
better understand the studio processes that created them. For example, the use of
cross-correlation to create a score that unpicks the cacophony of the samples
used in 'Operattack', or the use of time-scale analysis to depict, with greater
visual clarity than a spectrogram, the pitch transpositions of sampled material.
These bespoke adaptations have been used alongside more established tools for
music information retrieval, such as tempo trackers and chromagrams, to
provide a comprehensive picture (both literally and figuratively) of the signals
that comprise the text of this album. This is important since, as has been
demonstrated through their use, *Slave to the Rhythm*'s form and content have
much to with post hoc manipulations of material at this 'signal level', in
addition to those that are due to the songwriting and performance processes.

In particular, these newer tools for musical signal analysis, alongside more established visualisations such as scores depicting pitch and rhythm, enable a set of core materials to be identified and followed. The distribution of the components of this set, sometimes varied and sometimes unchanged, can then be observed and the form that the whole piece takes becomes clearer. *Slave to the Rhythm* is a tightly integrated work, but it is more than a collection of remixes, despite Horn's own description of the album as 'really an overblown twelve-inch' (Horn in Cunningham, 1998, pp. 308–9). The range of material and its variation goes far beyond, for example, the remixes that he created for the various twelve-inch singles ('Annihilation', 'Carnage', 'Hibakusha', 'Surrender' etc.) for Frankie Goes to Hollywood's 'Two Tribes' (Frankie Goes to Hollywood, 1984). The ostinato that is common to two middle movements is not present in either of the two single releases (which are based on the two outer movements), nor is it ever heard against the go-go groove that appears in various forms in much of the rest of the record. All of this places *Slave* in an unusual position between a large-scale multimovement work and an album of remixes. The extent of variation between pieces, and the different levels at which that variation occurs, makes *Slave* a fascinating and unique crossing between popular and classical form. When coupled with its cultural context, the intersections between popular music (with its emerging practice of direct quotation, via sampling technology) and filmmaking and photography, the gender fluidity of Jones herself, the album can be seen as a crossing between many important and varied strands in the culture and technology of its time.

References

Adorno, T. (1941). On Popular Music. *Studies in Philosophy and Social Science*, **9**, 17–48.

Advanced Music Systems (1978). *DMX15-80 User Manual*. Burnley: Advanced Music Systems.

Afrika Bambaataa and The Soul Sonic Force (1982) *Planet Rock* (7" single). New York: Tommy Boy Records (catalogue: TB 823–7).

Allinson, R. and Levine, S. (2006). *The Record Producers: Trevor Horn*. BBC Radio 6 Music, 17 April.

Ampex (1971). *AG-500 Series Price Schedule*. http://lcweb2.loc.gov/master/mbrs/ recording_preservation/manuals/AmpexAG-500Recorder-Reproducer pricesched(1971).pdf.

Angus, J. and Howard, D. (2009). *Acoustics and Psychoacoustics*, 5th ed. Oxford: Focal Press.

Anniss, M. (2016). J. J. Jeczalik: An Interview with the Fairlight Master. *Red Bull Music Academy*. https://daily.redbullmusicacademy.com/2016/11/jj-jeczalik-interview.

Anonymous (1983). Synclavier II, Part 1. *Electronics and Music Maker*, February 1983, 64–7.

Aphex Twin (1999). $\Delta M_i^{-1} = -\alpha \sum D_i[\eta][\sum F_{ji}[\eta-1]+\text{Fext}_i [\eta^{-1}]]$, *Windowlicker* (12" single). Sheffield: Warp Records (catalogue: WAP105).

Bass, H., Sutherland, C., Zuckerwar, A., Blackstock, D. and Hester, D. (1995). Atmospheric Absorption of Sound: Further Developments. *Journal of the Acoustical Society of America*, **97**(1), 680–3.

BBC Engineering (1963). Reverberation Plate EMT-140. *Miscellaneous Sound Equipment*. Technical Instruction S.9. www.bbceng.info/ti/eqpt/EMT140.pdf.

Beato, R. (2019). How Computers Ruined Rock Music. www.youtube.com/ watch?v=AFaRIW-wZlw.

Bennet, S. (2019). *Modern Records, Maverick Methods: Technology and Process in Popular Music Record Production 1978–2000*. New York: Bloomsbury Academic.

Blesser, B. (1971). Applying Digital Technology to Audio: Delay, Transmission, Storage and Other Forms of Processing. *The 41st Audio Engineering Society Convention*, paper number 826.

Brewster, B. and Broughton, F. (2018). Making Musical History: Arthur Baker and Electro in 1980s New York. *Red Bull Music Academy*. https://daily .redbullmusicacademy.com/2018/01/arthur-baker-interview.

Born, Georgina. (2009). Afterword; Recording: From Reproduction to Representation to Remediation. In Nicholas Cook, Eric Clarke, Daniel Leech-Wilkinson, and John Rink (eds.), *The Cambridge Companion to Recorded Music*, 286–304. Cambridge: Cambridge University Press.

Borwick, J. (1990). *Microphones: Theory and Practice*. Oxford: Focal Press.

Broccoli, A. and Wilson, M. (Prod.) (1985). *A View to a Kill*. Eon Productions film.

Burns, T. (2013). Tom Moulton. *Red Bull Music Academy*. www.redbullmusi cacademy.com/lectures/tom-moulton.

Buskin, R. (2013). 'Prince "Kiss"'. *Sound on Sound*. www.soundonsound.com/ sos/jun13/articles/classic-tracks-0613.htm.

Cambridge Dictionary. Culture. https://dictionary.cambridge.org/dictionary/ english/culture.

Chester, A. (1970). Second Thoughts on a Rock Aesthetic: The Band. *New Left Review*, **62**, 78–9.

Chowning, J. (1973). The Synthesis of Complex Audio Spectra by Means of Frequency Modulation. *Journal of the Audio Engineering Society*, **21**(7), 526–34.

Cook, N. (2013). *Beyond the Score*. Oxford: Oxford University Press.

Cunningham, M. (1998). *Good Vibrations: A History of Record Production*. London: Sanctuary.

Danielsen, A. (2010). Continuity and Break: James Brown's 'Funky Drummer'. https://edoc.hu-berlin.de/handle/18452/21060.

Davis, H. (1996). A History of Sampling. *Organised Sound*, **1**(1), 3–11.

Dockwray, R. and Moore, A. (2010). Configuring the Sound-Box 1965–72. *Popular Music*, **29**(2), 181–97.

Dolby, R. (1986). The Spectral Recording Process. *Audio Engineering Society Convention*, preprint 2431.

Edwards, G. (n.d.). *Seal* (Debut album) remixed/editted [sic] version. http:// futureloveparadise.co.uk/anthology/disc-album/seal1edit.html

Eno, B. (2017). The Studio as Compositional Tool. In C. Cox and D. Warner (eds.), *Audio Culture*, 127–30. London: Bloomsbury Academic.

E.U. (1985). *E.U. Freeze*. 4th and Broadway (catalogue 12 GOGO 3).

Flint, T. (2000). Mike Thorne: The Stereo Society, *Sound on Sound*. www .soundonsound.com/people/mike-thorne-stereo-society.

Frankie Goes to Hollywood (1984). *Welcome to the Pleasure Dome* (various formats). London: ZTT (e.g. catalogue: ZTAS 7).

Frankie Goes to Hollywood (1984). *Two Tribes* (various 12" single releases). London: ZTT (catalogue: 12 ZTAS 3 'Annihilation' and 'Surrender', XZTAS 3 'Carnage' and 'Surrender', XZIP 1 'Hibakusha').

Frith, S. (1998). *Performing Rites: On the Value of Popular Music.* Cambridge, MA: Harvard University Press.

Gardner, J. (2012). Interview: Peter Vogel. www.rnz.co.nz/concert/pro grammes/hopefulmachines/20131119.

Gilby, P. (1986). The Synclavier. *Sound on Sound*, May 1986, 12–16.

Glen, J. (2001). *For My Eyes Only.* London: Batsford.

Goude, J.-P. (1981). *Jungle Fever.* London: Quarto Books.

Goude, J.-P. (1983). *White and Black* [colour photograph]. www.jeanpaul goude.com/en/archives/grace-jones.

Greenslade, R. (1993). All about Lissajous Figures. *The Physics Teacher*, **31**, 364–70.

Hammond, R (1987). Peter Gabriel: Behind the Mask. *Sound on Sound.* January 1987, 40–5.

Hardcastle, P. (1985). *19.* London: Chrysalis Records (catalogue CHSR 2860).

Harness, D. (2008). *The Rhythm.* Oakland, CA: Moulton Records (no catalogue number). Available at www.beatport.com/track/the-rhythm-original-mix/ 7717910.

Harrison, A. (2010). Tuum Raider. www.zttaat.com/article.php?title=1021.

Jackson, M. (1982). *Thriller.* New York: Epic Records (catalogue QE 38112).

Jensen, K. and Herbert, D. (2016). Evaluation and Prediction of Harmonic Complexity Across 76 Years of Billboard 100 Hits. In R. Kronland-Martinet, M. Aramaki and S. Ystad, (eds.), *Music, Mind and Embodiment*, 283–96. Berlin: Springer.

Jones, G. (1980). *Warm Leatherette.* London: Island Records (catalogue ILPS 9592).

Jones, G. (1981). *Nightclubbing.* London: Island Records (catalogue 203 481).

Jones, G. (1982). *Living My Life.* London: Island Records (catalogue ILPS 9722).

Jones, G. (1985a). *Slave to the Rhythm* (7" single). London: Island Records/ ZTT (catalogue IS 206).

Jones, G. (1985b). *Slave to the Rhythm* (12" single). London: Island Records/ ZTT (catalogue 12IS 206).

Jones, G. (1985c). *Slave to the Rhythm* (album), 1st ed. London: Island Records/ ZTT (e.g. vinyl disk: catalogue Grace-1).

Jones, G. (1987). *Slave to the Rhythm*, 2nd ed. London: Island Records/ZTT (e.g. vinyl disk: catalogue ISSP 4011).

Jones, G. (2015). *I'll Never Write My Memoirs.* London: Simon & Schuster.

Lacasse, S. (2000). 'Listen to My Voice': The Evocative Power of Vocal Staging in Recorded Rock Music and Other Forms of Vocal Expression. PhD thesis, Laval University.

Lartillot, O. and Toiviainen, P. (2007). A Matlab Toolbox for Musical Feature Extraction from Audio. *Proceedings of the 10th International Conference on Digital Audio Effects*, 237–44. Bordeaux: University of Bordeaux.

Lavengood, M. (2017). A New Approach to the Analysis of Timbre. PhD thesis, City University of New York.

Lenhoff, A. and Robertson, D. (2019). *Classic Keys: Keyboard Sounds That Launched Rock Music*. Austin: University of Texas Press.

Liaisons, D. (1992). *The Rhythm,* appears on *Submerged in Sound*. Belgium: USA Import Records (catalogue USACD 10.133).

Lindvall, H. (2012). Behind the Music: Turning a Studio Performance into Recorded Magic. *The Guardian*, 29 March.

Long, P. (2012). *The History of the NME: High Times and Low Lives at the World's Most Famous Music Magazine*. London: Portico.

Lornell, K. and Stephenson, C. (2009). *The Beat: Go-Go Music from Washington, D.C.* Jackson: University Press of Mississippi.

Magritte, R. (1929). *The Treachery of Images* [painting]. Los Angeles County Museum of Art.

Mastergroove (2012). *Anialate*, appears on *Fine Groove*. Southampton: Kode5 Recordings. Available (as *Annihilate*) at https://mastergroove1.bandcamp .com/track/annihilate.

McCallum, J. (2022). *Memory Prices 1957+*. www.jcmit.net/memoryprice .htm.

McLeod, K. and Dicola, P. (2011). *Creative License: The Law and Culture of Digital Sampling*. Durham, NC: Duke University Press.

Metheny, P. (1989). *Electric Counterpoint*, appears on Kronos Quartet and Metheny, P. *Different Trains/Electric Counterpoint*. New York: Nonesuch Records (catalogue: 9–79176–2).

Michael Viner's Incredible Bongo Band (1973). *Apache,* appears on *Bongo Rock*. Los Angeles, CA: MGM Records (catalogue 2315 255).

Middleton, R. (1983). 'Play It Again Sam': Some Notes on the Productivity of Repetition in Popular Music. *Popular Music*, **3**, 235–70.

Middleton, R. (1999). Form. In B. Horner and T. Swiss, eds., *Key Terms in Popular Music and Culture*, 141–55. Oxford: Blackwell.

Milner, G. (2009). *Perfecting Sound Forever*. London: Granta.

Moore, A. (2007). Review of *The Producer as Composer*, by Virgil Moorefield. *Twentieth Century Music*, **4**(1), 127–9.

Moore, A. (2001). *Rock: The Primary Text*. Aldershot: Ashgate Publishing.

Moore, R. (2008). *My Word Is My Bond*. London: O'Mara.

Moorefield, V. (2005). *The Producer As Composer*. Cambridge, MA: MIT Press.

Morton, D. (2006). *Sound Recording: The Life Story of a Technology.* Baltimore, MD: Johns Hopkins University Press.

Murphy, M. and Anstey, R. (2020). Reimagining Robb: The Sound of the World's First Sample-Based Electronic Musical Instrument circa 1927. *Audio Engineering Society Convention.* e-Brief 585.

Murray, C. (1984). Sermon From the Savoy. *New Musical Express,* 29 September. https://paola1chi.blogspot.com/2019/09/sermon-from-savoy-interview-by-charles.html.

New York Times News Service (1987). Dolby Fights Digital Recording, But Quietly. *Chicago Tribune,* 5 December.

Niles, R. (2009). Interview with Trevor Horn. www.youtube.com/watch?v=AFaRIW-wZlw.

Nordhaus, W. (2001). The Progress of Computing. Cowles Foundation Discussion Paper 1324. New Haven, CT: Cowles Foundation.

Patten, D. (2019). Interview with Ian McShane. www.youtube.com/watch?v=l7kFN1xN6ic.

Penman, I. (1985). The Annihilation of Rhythm. Spoken word introduction to G. Jones, *Slave to the Rhythm.* London: Island Records/ZTT.

Presley, E. (1954). *Blue Moon of Kentucky.* [7" single]. Memphis: Sun Records (catalogue 209).

Prince (1986). 'Kiss', *Parade.* [Compact Disc]. Minneapolis, MN: Paisley Park CD.

Propaganda (1985). *The Murder of Love,* appears on *A Secret Wish.* London: Ztt (catalogue ZTTIQ 3).

Red Princess (1993). *You Make Me Feel So Good (Call Mix).* Mouscron: Diki Records (catalogue DIKI 50.12.60).

Renevolution (2019). Frankie Goes to Hollywood 'Slave to the Rhythm' (1984/85). www.youtube.com/watch?v=HB4gBtMpUIs

Roads, C. (1996). *The Computer Music Tutorial.* Cambridge, MA: MIT Press.

Rogers, G. (1983). *The Nature of Engineering.* London: The MacMillan Press.

Rumsey, F. and McCormick, T. (2014). *Sound and Recording,* 7th ed. Oxford: Focal Press.

Sato, N. (1973). PCM Recorder: A New Type of Audio Magnetic Tape Recorder. *Journal of the Audio Engineering Society,* **21**(7), 542–8.

Sauers, J. (2009). Why Photograph a Black Woman in a Cage? *Jezebel.* http://jezebel.com/5337618/why-photograph-a-black-woman-in-a-cage.

Schroeder, M. (1979). Binaural Dissimilarity and Optimum Ceilings for Concert Halls: More Lateral Sound Diffusion. *Journal of the Acoustical Society of America,* **65**(4), 958–63.

Siedenburg, K. and McAdams, S. (2017). Four Distinctions for the Auditory 'Wastebasket' of Timbre. *Frontiers of Psychology,* **8**, Article 1747.

Smith, J. (2011). *Spectral Audio Signal Processing*. Stanford: W3 K Publishing.

The South Bank Show (1982). ITV, 31 October.

Steinski and The Mass Media (1986). *And the Motorcade Sped On*. New York: Tommy Boy Records (catalogue TB885).

Studer Professional Audio AG (1993). *A820 Operating Instructions*. Zurich: Studer.

Tagg, P. (n.d.). Glossary of Terms. https://tagg.org/articles/ptgloss.html.

Tagg, P. (2013). *Music's Meanings*. Huddersfield: The Mass Media Music Scholars' Press.

The Art of Noise (1999). *The Seduction of Claude Debussy*. London: ZTT (catalogue: ztt130 cd).

The KLF (1990). *Chillout*. London: KLF Communications (catalogue: JAMS LP5).

The Orb (1989). *A Huge Ever Growing Pulsating Brain That Rules From The Centre Of The Ultraworld*. London: WAU! Mr Modo Records(catalogue: MWS 017 T).

The Orb (1990). *Little Fluffy Clouds*. London: WAU! Mr Modo Records (catalogue: BLR 33 T).

The Rolling Stones (1965). *(I Can't Get No) Satisfaction*. London: Decca (catalogue: F.12220).

The Winstons (1969). *Amen, Brother/Color Him, Father*. New York: Metromedia Records (catalogue MMS-117).

Tingen, P. (1987). Steve Lipson: The Price of Fame. *Music Technology*, May, 54–8.

Tingen, P. (1996). Fairlight: The Whole Story. *Audio Media*, January, 48–55.

Urayama, K., Ishiwata, K., Shirako, Y., Kawachi, H. and Kondo, T. (1988). Advances in DASH Format Multi-Channel Recording. *Audio Engineering Society Convention*, Preprint 2736.

Walters, B. (2015a). Interview with Bruce Woolley. www.brucewoolleyhq.com/pitchfork-interview.html.

Walters, B. (2015b). As Black as I Am, as Much as I Can: The Queer History of Grace Jones. *The Pitchfork Review*, August . https://pitchfork.com/features/from-the-pitchfork-review/9708-as-much-as-i-can-as-black-as-i-am-the-queer-history-of-grace-jones/.

Warner, T. (2003). *Pop Music Technology and Creativity: Trevor Horn and the Digital Revolution*. London: Routledge.

Watkinson, J. (2000). *The Art of Digital Audio*. Oxford: Focal Press.

Weber, W. (1999). The History of Musical Canon. In N. Cook and M. Everist (eds.), *Rethinking Music*, 336–55. Oxford: Oxford University Press.

Whitesell, L. (2008). *The Music of Joni Mitchell*. New York: Oxford University Press.

Wishart, T. (1977). Musical Writing, Musical Speaking. In J. Shepherd, P. Virden, G. Vulliamy, and T. Wishart (eds.), *Whose Music? A Sociology of Musical Languages*, 125–53. London: Latimer.

Wishart, T. and Virden, P. (1977). Some Observations on the Social Stratification of Twentieth-Century Music. In J. Shepherd, P. Virden, G. Vulliamy and T. Wishart (eds.), *Whose Music? A Sociology of Musical Languages*, 155–77. London: Latimer.

Zagorski-Thomas, S. (2014). *The Musicology of Record Production*. Cambridge: Cambridge University Press.

For my parents, who gave me everything I needed.

Cambridge Elements ≡

Popular Music

Rupert Till

University of Huddersfield

Rupert Till is Professor of Music at the University of Huddersfield, UK, Associate Dean International in his faculty and Director of the Confucius Institute at the University. He has research interests in popular music and sound archaeology. He is Chair of the International Association for the Study of Popular Music IASPM, and a committee member of the UK and Ireland Branch. He directed Huddersfield activities within the EU funded European Music Archaeology Project, (2013–18), and has been Principal Investigator for two AHRC/EPSRC grants. He studied composition with Gavin Bryars, Christopher Hobbs, Katharine Norman, and George Nicholson. He continues to write electronica and perform under the name 'Professor Chill'.

About the Series

Elements in Popular Music explores popular music from a variety of perspectives, including musically focused and cultural studies approaches. It addresses music creation, performance, recording and production, and the music industries across a wide range of genres, artists and works, showcasing the vibrant diversity of the music and its practitioners.

Cambridge Elements ᐧ

Popular Music

Elements in the Series

Rock Guitar Virtuosos: Advances in Electric Guitar Playing, Technology And Culture
Jan-Peter Herbst & Alexander Paul Vallejo

The Crossings
Jeremy J. Wells

A full series listing is available at: www.cambridge.org/epop